The Month of St. Joseph:
Prayers and Practices for Each Day of March in Imitation of the Virtues of St. Joseph

by
Most Rev. M. de Langalerie

Translated from the French by a
Sister of St. Joseph

Supplemental Material by
Janet P. McKenzie, OCDS

Biblio Resource Publications, Inc.
108½ S. Moore Street
Bessemer, MI 49911

Published by Biblio Resource Publications, Inc.
108½ South Moore Street, Bessemer, MI 49911
www.BiblioResource.com
info@biblioresource.com

A **R**ead **A**loud **C**urriculum **E**nrichment Product
www.RACEforHeaven.com

Cover Art © Madeleine Openshaw - Fotolia.com

Printed in the United States of America

The Author's Preface

In the preface of *An Introduction to the Devout Life*, St. Francis de Sales, anticipating the reproach of having devoted to that work more time than the care of a diocese could have allowed him, replied, with the great St. Denis, that the perfecting of souls belongs principally to bishops, and their time could not be more usefully employed than in writing books the reading of which might animate souls to a desire of perfection. These words, even more than the success of the holy author of *The Devout Life*, justify our own desire in the writing of this work. To have St. Joseph honored and imitated by the faithful, to propose to them the meditation of his virtues and the practice of devotion to him, appears to us an excellent means towards promoting the good of souls, in conformity with the desire of St. Denis and the idea of St. Francis de Sales.

We are happy in the hope that even after our death this little work will inspire many souls with holy sentiments, generous resolutions, love of God and of their neighbor. We recommend the spirit of sacrifice and the obligation which binds us to the practice of self-denial and Christian mortification. Each day we indicate a different means of bringing home to ourselves this important teaching of the Gospel; and the practices which we propose need not so engage us as to interfere with duties towards those claiming our attention. The great tendency of the age is a desire of comfort, ease, self-indulgence, and independence. Such being directly opposed to the spirit of Christianity, no effort should be spared in destroying it in ourselves and averting its dread consequences from others.

The Month of St. Joseph

The month of St. Joseph [March] occurs in Lent, during which season the duty of the mortification of our passions and natural inclinations is more frequently recalled to our minds. These exercises for the month of St. Joseph must not conflict with those of Lent. We should participate in parish activities and attend the particular instructions given there. These exercises in honor of St. Joseph may form a supplement of devotion, which will be the more meritorious and profitable to our souls as we will be the more exact in the fulfillment of the important duties imposed on us by the Church during the holy season of Lent. Nothing can replace the admirable practice of attending Mass and parish educational opportunities and of reading the daily Gospel. The duty of giving edification rests on each and every one of us. We should bear in mind that each parish is a family, the members of which are united by faith, and mutually owe good example to one another.

Having opened by using his apology, so now we conclude in the words of our beloved St. Francis de Sales: "A practiced flower-girl so skillfully varies the hue and mixture that with the same flowers she arranges a great variety of bouquets; thus the Holy Spirit disposes with as much diversity the instruction of devotion, which is given us through the tongues and pens of His servants; that, although the doctrine be the same, the mode of treating it differs according to the several methods in which they are composed." Here is our bouquet, which, though much inferior to that of St. Francis de Sales, we present with a heart deeply devoted to the salvation of souls. Amen.

Most Rev. M. de Langalerie,
Archbishop of Auch
1874

The Editor's Preface

As Archbishop de Langalerie points out in this book, St. Teresa of Avila was instrumental in fostering devotion to the foster-father of Jesus. My exposure to her writings began with my spiritual formation as a secular Carmelite in 2002. On October 27, 2009—the day I professed my definitive promises as a secular Carmelite—I purchased a remembrance of that special day from the gift shop of the Monastery of the Holy Cross in Iron Mountain, Michigan, where I made my profession—a wooden statue of St. Joseph the Worker crafted by one of the Sisters there. This statue sat on my bedroom dresser for almost a year.

During that year, we had a house that was unsuccessfully listed with a real estate broker. In October of 2010, we decided to make a novena to St. Joseph for the intention of selling this house. We dutifully buried a small plastic statue of St. Joseph in the house's yard and brought the larger, wooden statue to a place of honor in the living room. As evidence of the love and power of St. Joseph, we privately sold this house—within a month and at our asking price—to a couple who lived six hundred miles away. The plastic statue was retrieved, and both statues remain on display in our living room. Thank you, St. Joseph!

My journey to St. Joseph began in earnest. To fulfill a promise I had made to him, I began the work of compiling a children's read-aloud book in his honor. On October 15, 2011 (the feast day of St. Teresa of Avila), *Devotion to St. Joseph: Read-Aloud Stories, Poems, and Prayers for Catholic Children* was published. (See page 155 for more details.)

However, in the summer of that year, I had received a request from an aspiring Carmelite in our parish book club to read a book on St. Joseph. As I had difficulty finding what I deemed a suitable book, I was determined that I would publish one that would inspire others to imitate the life of this great saint. I humbly pray that this re-published edition of Archbishop M. de Langalerie's *The Month of St. Joseph* accomplishes this goal.

As I bring this book honoring St. Joseph back into publication, I am indebted to many people: Therese *of the Child Jesus and of the Holy Face* Bartlett OCDS for her gift of money and request that I buy "something special" at the Carmelite gift shop, the Carmelite Sisters of the Monastery of the Holy Cross for the beautiful statue of St. Joseph as well as their continued prayers and sacrifices for our secular community and the Church, Mary Anne Kimball for her indirect request for this book, my beloved husband Jim for his patience with my quirky writing hours and his continual spiritual support, and—of course—St. Joseph for his ever-faithful assistance in our earthly toils and dedication to our eternal salvation.

My husband and I continue to pray to St. Joseph daily for his intercession in our various business endeavors as well as his spiritual assistance. As he continues to bless us, I am assured that he will bless all who earnestly implore his help. While I believe that the prayers and practices of this book will inspire each individual reader, I also know the power of reading aloud together. Please consider reading *The Month of St. Joseph* aloud with your spouse or older children; discuss it together and work to transform your lives in imitation of our powerful patron, St. Joseph.

In gratitude to St. Joseph for his many favors,
Janet *of My Jesus Most Merciful* McKenzie OCDS
February 2, 2012
Feast of the Presentation

Contents

Contents

The Month of St. Joseph

Eve of the First Day
"Go to Joseph."

THESE words were addressed by Pharaoh to his subjects (Genesis 41:55), who, when harassed by famine and distress, implored his aid. And we introduce them at the beginning of these pious exercises in order to establish a striking resemblance between the two patriarchs who, separated by an interval of seventeen centuries, have borne the glorious name of Joseph.

First Resemblance: *The trials to which they were subjected* — Those of the first Joseph are so well known that there needs be no repetition of them. [See Genesis 37 and 39-45.] Pursued by the hatred of his brothers, and traitorously sold into slavery by them, he relied on God alone as the protector of his weakness and defender of his innocence. The second Joseph, though a descendant of the kings of Judah, lived in obscurity and poverty bordering on want. An outcast in Bethlehem, obliged to flee to Egypt, and abandoned by men, he was supported in his trials by his confidence, love, and fidelity towards God.

Let us learn from the example of these two great patriarchs how to endure the trials that accompany us on our journey through life, and let us be animated by the influence of this thought: God is with me, He loves and protects me. "If God is for us, who can be against us?" (Romans 8:31)

Second Resemblance: *The nature of their duties, and the manner in which these duties were fulfilled* — The first

1

Joseph was a faithful servant in the house of Potiphar, a prudent and upright minister in the court of Pharaoh. Neither the allurements of pleasure, nor the fear of chastisements nor the treacherous fascinations of human grandeur could shake his fidelity. Ever faithful in his duty towards God, he was likewise dutiful to his master, occupying himself with the care of his own soul in preference to all other interests. The second Joseph was also a most faithful minister in a royalty far more exalted and important than the one with which the well-beloved son of Jacob was honored. Charged by the Almighty, the Eternal King of ages, to be the protector of the life, and guardian of the virginal purity of the noble Mary, Mother of God, he was likewise entrusted with the guardianship of the infancy and youth of the Savior, thus bearing the relation of foster-father to the Redeemer of the human race.

My God! What a beautiful, grand, and sublime mystery! St. Joseph fulfilled his ministry agreeably to the wishes of His Sovereign, who Himself renders testimony to Joseph's justice when in the Gospel He says, "Joseph was a just man" (Matthew 1:19, Douay-Rheims translation). But if Joseph was a just and—by consequence—a faithful and prudent guardian of the two inestimable treasures that were confided to him, it is because, as the Scriptures express it, "He hath not taken his soul in vain" (Psalm 24:4, Douay-Rheims translation). He knew that an account should be rendered of the manner in which he discharged his duty as protector of the virgin Mother and her divine Son.

Each one of us has a mission to fulfill, a ministry of some kind to exercise, and we should learn fidelity from the example of St. Joseph. Our eternal salvation depends on the faithful discharge of our duties. The saving of our own soul would be in itself a ministry, but, alas, how many other souls depend also on us! We should, then, while endeavoring to save our own souls, do all in our power towards the saving of souls confided to our care, so that at death these sweet words may be addressed to us: "Well done, my good and faithful servant. Since you were faithful in small matters, I will give you great responsibilities. Come, share your master's joy" (Matthew 25:23).

Third Resemblance: *Their connection with Jesus Christ* — The first Joseph, in his trials and afflictions as well as in his triumphs, is regarded as one of the most striking images of Jesus Christ. It was not without a mysterious coincidence that Pharaoh gave him a name signifying *savior of the world*. Though the second Joseph did not himself bear the name "Savior of Mankind," he had the privilege of giving it to Him by whom alone it was merited.

He was appointed protector of the person of Jesus, His guardian and foster-father. Jesus redeemed the world, and Joseph guarded and protected Jesus. We have said that he proved himself as a just man and faithful servant in his great and elevated mission; but we must add here that it was through the intimate and direct influence of the Savior that he accomplished the designs of God, and arrived at the perfection of his ministry. He was one of the first and most admirable imitators of the great Model, whom he closely contemplated. The spirit of the Savior became his spirit, whereby he attained that new birth mentioned by Nicodemus, which consists of divesting ourselves of our own will, combating our inclinations, and subjecting our passions to reason and religion that our lives may be in accordance with the spirit of Jesus Christ.

The first Joseph felt this influence in an indirect manner, as all the just of the Old Testament participated in the grace of the Redemption, though in a way constrained by the fact that the institutions of the old law were not in themselves perfect. Dating from St. John the Baptist, the Blessed Virgin, and St. Joseph, the spirit of the new law spreads itself with a plenitude and rapidity that manifests the presence of the Incarnate Word.

Have we entered into the spirit of Jesus Christ by our fidelity to His law and conformity with His divine will?

"Go to Joseph," we say. God, the Sovereign Master, invites you to Joseph in confiding the Author of grace to his care.

"Go to Joseph," says the Holy Church; and it is not with her as of old with ungrateful Egypt, who, after a few centuries, had forgotten the memory of her benefactor. The Church, on the contrary, attaches itself by a closer tie to the remembrance of St. Joseph as the years from the period of his mortal life recede. Instead of the material food with which the ancient patriarch fed the Egyptians, Joseph has received and guarded for us the life-giving Bread descended from heaven to nourish and sanctify our souls. Like Jesus and Mary, you must repair the sinful outrages and blasphemies against the majesty of God. Where is the virginal purity of Mary—where the glory of St. Joseph— when Jesus is spoken of by unbelievers as an ordinary man, and His birth not regarded as a miracle of the power of God? *Go to Joseph.* The first Joseph demanded the Egyptians to sacrifice and abandon their individual fortunes for the common good; and our Joseph asks you to divest yourself of your imperfections—to replace them with the love of Jesus.

Prayer

HOLY St. Joseph! Behold at your feet our humble souls, ardently desiring to profit by the graces attached to your example and intercession. We pray that during this month our souls may be nourished by the study of your virtuous life. Guardian of Jesus, be our protector and our guide. Pray for us, and present our prayers—purified by your own prayers—to the Sacred Heart of Jesus and to the Immaculate Heart of Mary. Amen.

Resolutions

1. During the course of the day, recall to your mind the preceding reflections.
2. Enter into the spirit of the holy season of Lent and comply with the requirements of the Church.
3. Do not seek dispensation from the Lenten fast without sufficient cause.
4. Recite the Our Father and Hail Mary once, and "St. Joseph, pray for us" three times.

Aspiration

"Go to St. Joseph."

Scripture Verse

"If God is for us, who can be against us?" (Romans 8:31)

Daily Meditation

"Each one of us has a mission to fulfill, a ministry of some kind to exercise, and we should learn fidelity from the example of St. Joseph. Our eternal salvation depends on the faithful discharge of our duties. The saving of our own soul would be in itself a ministry, but, alas, how many other souls depend also on us! We should, then, while endeavoring to save our own souls, do all in our power towards the saving of souls confided to our care, so that at death these sweet words may be addressed to us: "Well done, my good and faithful servant. Since you were faithful in small matters, I will give you great responsibilities. Come, share your master's joy" (Matthew 25:23)."

First Day
St. Joseph, Spouse of the Blessed Virgin

FIRST Point: The first and most essential attribute of St. Joseph is that of Spouse of the Blessed Virgin Mary. He is only the foster-father of Jesus Christ, but he is the spouse of the Virgin Mother of God. He was chosen from among thousands—from among tens of thousands—from among all men—to be honored by this glorious privilege. A pious tradition relates that when the choice of a husband was imposed on the Blessed Virgin, her guardian called together all her relations of the race of David and tribe of Judah. Joseph came among the others who aspired to the honor; but his modesty kept him at a distance until the Almighty, by a miracle, decided in his favor.

Each candidate left an almond-tree rod in the Temple in the evening,, and the next day the dry and withered branch of Joseph, like that which of old secured the priesthood to Aaron, was found green and blossomed with fragrant flowers—graceful symbols of the virtues that had fixed the choice of God on Joseph to be the guardian of the most precious treasure, after the humanity of Jesus Christ, that earth ever possessed. That treasure belonged to God and to men, but in a particular manner to St. Joseph; for the sacred tie that bound the affections united the lives of Joseph and Mary. Let us admire this privilege and congratulate our glorious protector on its possession.

Recall to mind the words he so frequently addressed to himself: Spouse of Mary—what an honor! What a grace! What a responsibility!

Second Point: One practical reflection is the mainspring of the doctrine contained in the first point of this meditation. To Mary, Joseph owed the honor of his close relationship to Jesus. He was regarded as the foster-father of Jesus only by his title of spouse of Mary, and the graces and privileges granted him were essential to his connections with her. This fact, important in its application to all Christians, is particularly so to us. Our relations with Jesus should be through Mary, since every good comes to us from Him through her. By His birth from her, He became our brother, and we became her children by the adoption made at the foot of the Cross on Calvary. Let us, then, go to Jesus through Mary, and to Mary through our glorious protector, St. Joseph. If we pray to him, he will obtain for us, by his intercession with Jesus and Mary, an abundance of heavenly graces emanating from the loving heart of Jesus and the maternal hands of our loving mother, Mary.

Third Point: What an honor! Let us repeat these words in unison with St. Joseph congratulating himself on the glorious title which united him to Mary. What an honor, what a responsibility, but also what a grace! These three words may be applied to all who have received vocations to leave all and follow Christ. Priests and religious should frequently entertain this salutary reflection; what a responsibility rests on those favored by God and honored with this grace of graces!

Christians should ponder these words, and apply them to themselves. The vocation to Christianity by baptism is the greatest and most admirable of all graces. What an honor to be a child of God and of His Church, brother and co-heir of Jesus Christ, and the temple of the Holy Spirit! But, alas! What a responsibility to be the possessor of precious treasures carried in frail vases; for baptism has not freed us from the effects of concupiscence [or the tendency of our human nature to sin as a result of original sin].

The fears awakened by this responsibility may, however, be removed by the thought of the superabundant graces which flow from the mercy and love of God—graces that are intended not only to be applied to our own souls, but also are designed and should be made profitable to the many souls whose salvation and eternal happiness depend on us.

Prayer

O GLORIOUS St. Joseph, my holy protector, obtain that my soul may derive benefit from this first meditation. You who did so often guide Jesus in His infancy, direct me and protect me during these days which I offer and consecrate to you. Lead me to Mary and to Jesus, and teach me to know and love them more fully and ardently. Amen.

Resolutions

1. During the course of the day, recall to your mind the preceding reflections.
2. Restrain curiosity.
3. Accept, without manifesting ill-humor, the annoyances that result from the exercises of duty and charity.
4. Do not eat between meals. [Restrain concupiscence.]
5. Recite both the Our Father and Hail Mary once, and "St. Joseph, pray for us" three times.

Aspiration

"St. Joseph, spouse of the Blessed Virgin Mary, pray for us."

Scripture Verse

". . . we are children of God, and if children, then heirs, heirs of God and joint heirs with Christ, if only we suffer with him so that we may also be glorified with him." (Romans 8:16-17)

Daily Meditation

"Our relations with Jesus should be through Mary, since every good comes to us from Him through her. By His birth from her, He became our brother, and we became her children by the adoption made at the foot of the Cross on Calvary. Let us, then, go to Jesus through Mary, and to Mary through our glorious protector, St. Joseph. If we pray to him, he will obtain for us, by his intercession with Jesus and Mary, an abundance of heavenly graces emanating from the loving heart of Jesus and the maternal hands of our loving mother, Mary."

Second Day
St. Joseph, Foster-Father of Jesus Christ

ST. JOSEPH is not, it is true, the father of Jesus Christ according to nature; nevertheless, his office towards the Son of God gave him all the rights of paternity.

First Point: *God distinctly recognized the parental right of St. Joseph* — Previous to the advent of Christ, it was the design of Providence to conceal from the world and from Satan the coming of the Savior and His birth of a virgin; hence God willed that St. Joseph should be regarded as the father of our Lord. To manifest this design, all the rights and all the honors of paternity were accorded to him, and his heart was animated with parental love towards Jesus. As the gifts of God are never recalled, it follows that for all eternity St. Joseph will possess these privileges—a sweet and cherished thought for hearts devoted to the service of God! This is a solid and immovable foundation upon which to raise a tender and ardent affection to St. Joseph! These thoughts are clearly established, since heaven has confirmed, by a singular development, the extent of the glory of St. Joseph. Let our mind dwell on these three truths: God has given to St. Joseph, first, the honor of paternity towards our Lord; second, the rights of this paternity; and third, a most paternal affection for him. What precious gifts, rich in the wealth of power implied in their possession! What treasures of tenderness and bounty they place in the heart of St. Joseph!

Second Point: *St. Joseph's right of paternity is recognized by men* — That St. Joseph, during his life, was regarded as the foster-father of our divine Savior is proved

11

by the language of the Jews on various occasions. Is He not, say they, the son of Joseph, the son of the carpenter? (See Matthew 13:55.) These were, according to their idea, expressions of contempt for our Lord; they knew not that these words served to increase beyond measure the dignity and standing of His foster-father. They would have known this had the mystery of the Incarnation been revealed to them as it was to St. Joseph. But as their hearts were not prepared for this favor, the knowledge was not accorded them. St. Joseph held secret this revelation by the command of God. He loved this silence, inasmuch as it was to him a source of happiness to obey the God of mercy and truth. His title of father was universally recognized by his contemporaries, and he regarded it as an incomparable honor to be associated in this most intimate manner with the humiliations of the Savior. Of Jesus Christ they said: "This is the son of the carpenter." Of St. Joseph they might have said: "This is the father of the Galilean." Let us learn from this example that, when the wicked inflict outrages and persecutions on us, they serve to promote our honor and glory, providing we suffer them for God or in the cause of religion. We should rejoice to be deemed worthy of persecution for justice's sake. Let us pardon our persecutors, and love them, that our patience may triumph over their malice, and contribute to the eternal honor of the Christian faith. "Do not be conquered by evil but conquer evil with good" (Romans 12:21).

Third Point: *St. Joseph's right of paternity is manifested by the actions of our Lord: "He . . . was subject to them." (Luke 2:51, Douay-Rheims translation)* — This one sentence of the Gospel suffices to show that our Lord was subject to Joseph and to Mary as a son is subject to his parents. Jesus was regarded as the son of Joseph, as much by the respect, deference, and affection which He manifested toward His foster-father, as by all the other appearances that justify this title. And Jesus would not act a part. It was necessary that He should experience—let us speak clearly—that He should really feel for St. Joseph the sentiments that were expressed in His manner towards him. Jesus Christ, then, had for St. Joseph the heartfelt affection of the most tender, loving, respectful, and obedient of all sons. Let us congratulate St. Joseph on this filial tenderness that our Lord had for him. How many spiritual favors must have been given St. Joseph, and what an increase of virtue and merit must have been produced in him by the love of Jesus! A proof is hereby given us of the powerful protection of this great saint. "Were I master, what would I not do for my parents?" said a good son. Jesus Christ is Master, and during life He gave His foster-father virtue, which is more than all the riches and treasures of the earth; and now, in heaven, He gives him power.

Prayer

HOLY St. Joseph, foster-father of Jesus Christ, behold at your feet His brothers and sisters, and your children. Have for us the loving kindness of a father. Take from us the joys of home, family, and country, if their possession is detrimental to our souls; seek for us if we wander from the path traced out by your example; seek us until we hear your voice; receive our petitions; dry our tears; guard and grant that we may always be to you as was the divine Savior Himself—tender, submissive, and respectful. Amen.

Resolutions

1. During the course of the day, recall to mind the preceding reflections.
2. Endure cheerfully the inclemencies of the season.

3. Recite both the Our Father and Hail Mary once, and "St. Joseph, pray for us" three times.

Aspiration
"St. Joseph, foster-father of Jesus Christ, pray for us."

Scripture Verse
"Blessed are they who are persecuted for the sake of righteousness, for theirs is the kingdom of heaven." (Matthew 5:10)

Daily Meditation
"Let us learn from this example that, when the wicked inflict outrages and persecutions on us, they serve to promote our honor and glory, providing we suffer them for God or in the cause of religion. We should rejoice to be deemed worthy of persecution for justice's sake. Let us pardon our persecutors, and love them, that our patience may triumph over their malice, and contribute to the eternal honor of the Christian faith."

Third Day
St. Joseph, Model of Attention in Prayer

FIRST **Point:** *Necessity of prayer* — It is important to frequently recall to our minds that prayer is essential to the practice of all the virtues, to the avoidance of sin, and in general to the fulfillment of our duties. Prayer is necessary not only as a means of soliciting the graces needed for our souls, but also as an offering of gratitude, adoration, and love towards God, whose infinite bounty, goodness, and love demand this triple return on our part. Our Lord Himself taught us this manner of prayer and left us a most admirable form in the Our Father. Frequent prayer was recommended in the old law, and we see the exactitude with which the Pharisees observed this counsel; but what they did merely through ceremony St. Joseph, a true Israelite, fulfilled in a spirit of faith animated by love of God.

Second Point: *Essential qualities of prayer* — Prayer must be accompanied with confidence, humility, and fervor. Prayer is, in itself, an act of humility; for in soliciting favors from God, or when returning thanks for those already received, we find ourselves penetrated with a knowledge of our own unworthiness and misery, and our absolute dependence on God. This humility tends to increase our confidence in the goodness and mercy of God; and prayers uttered with confidence always receive the favor solicited, though for a time it may seem that Almighty God refuses to listen favorably to our petitions. Love, accompanied by fervor, is the third disposition that renders our prayers pleasing to God and effective in our advancement in perfection. "He who ceases to love ceases to pray," says St. Augustine. A few moments' meditation on these words would suffice to convince us of the importance of this most essential quality of prayer.

Third Point: *Prayer in common* — We will find our models in this exercise in the humble cottage at Nazareth. It cannot be deemed rash to assert that Jesus, Mary, and Joseph frequently practiced this holy exercise, nor can it be too much to consider Mary and Joseph as being the first to receive from the lips of Jesus that prayer which He Himself is the author. We are bound, after their example, to establish in our homes, not only the use of this prayer, but also family prayer, at least once per day; and if this usage has been already established in the family of which we are members, we should endeavor by every means in our power to introduce it into the homes of others. Nor should we content ourselves with merely reciting family prayers, but should, moreover, accustom ourselves to read daily passages from the Scriptures, the lives of the saints, *The Imitation of Christ*, the history of the Church, or some other work on religion or piety. Incredible advantages have been derived from the observance of these pious practices, not the least of which is the impression that it stamps on the mind of youth. Again, we see how pleasing is this practice to our Lord in the assurance He gives when He says, "Again, [amen], I say to you, if two of you agree on earth about anything for which they are to pray, it shall be granted to them by my heavenly Father" (Matthew 18:19).

Prayer

HOLY St. Joseph! Permit me to unite my prayers with those you offered up with Jesus and Mary. Obtain that I may become more attentive and more devout during prayer. You who are in a particular manner the patron of family prayer, bless those who unite here on earth in praising Jesus, whose protector you were, and obtain for them the graces needed for their salvation. Yes, dear patron, bless them, and bless me now as I implore your assistance. Amen.

Resolutions
1. During the course of the day, recall to mind the preceding reflections.
2. Pray often with confidence, humility, fervor, and love.
3. Pray both the Our Father and Hail Mary once and "St. Joseph, pray for us" three times.

Aspiration
"St. Joseph, model of attention in prayer, pray for us."

Scripture Verse
"Again, [amen], I say to you, if two of you agree on earth about anything for which they are to pray, it shall be granted to them by my heavenly Father." (Matthew 18:19)

Daily Meditation
"It is important to frequently recall to our minds that prayer is essential to the practice of all the virtues, to the avoidance of sin, and in general to the fulfillment of our duties. . . . Prayer must be accompanied with confidence, humility, and fervor."

Fourth Day
St. Joseph, Model of Interior Recollection

FIRST **Point:** The habit of prayer produces in the soul an interior recollection, which keeps the mind fixed on God, and prevents our being too absorbed in exterior occupations. One who has acquired this habit lives in the continual presence of the great Being who called him into existence; and, whether employed in laborious duties, or mingling in the busy scenes of life, he never loses sight of that one all-inspiring thought, beside which all earthly joys dwindle into nothingness. This is what we term the interior or meditative life. Let us consider how profound and tranquil must have been the life of St. Joseph, who, whether at work alone or with companions, had his heart and mind centered on God. We behold him ever the same; his noble and serene countenance bearing that indelible mark that the constant union of the soul with God always imprints. Here is our model. Let us endeavor, after his example, to acquire this interior recollection, which will enable us to overcome temptations, whatever be their nature or strength. Habitual prayer is the most effective means for obtaining this end; and, in order to aid those desiring to acquire this practice, we give two forms of prayer,

Second Point: The first form is ejaculatory prayers—short aspirations directed to God with all the fervor which the soul is capable. Occupying but a moment, they take from the evil one all power of depriving them of their effectiveness. They have, then, a greater influence over the heart of Jesus, forcing Him, as it were, to listen favorably, and grant our petitions. Such, for example, were the aspirations of a Vincent de Paul, a Teresa of Avila, a Francis

19

de Sales, a Magdalen de Pazzi, and many others. What St. Joseph's were we know not; but from a heart so just, so pure, and filled with the love of God as was his heart, aspirations ardent and fervent must have issued. Let us implore St. Joseph to obtain for us that our hearts may be animated with sentiments very much like his.

Third Point: *Mental prayer* — Mental prayer serves to unite our souls to God and aids in the practice of habitual recollection. When beginning this exercise, we should place ourselves in the presence of God, adore His infinite majesty, acknowledge our own weakness and misery, implore the assistance of the Holy Spirit, and reflect a few moments on the proposed subject. This subject may consist of one of the truths of religion, a good thought, a passage from a pious book, or from the Gospel or epistle of the day, a virtue to be acquired, or a vice to be overcome. The reflections made should dispose our souls to become worthy recipients of grace. Emotions of the heart succeed the reflection, and these, with affections of the will, are the most important parts of the meditation. The exercise is finished by taking a practical resolution for the day, which may be drawn from the subject on which we meditated, or it may be the correction of a predominant fault, or the avoidance of an occasion of sin; and, lastly, an aspiration should be chosen, to be repeated frequently during the day, so that it may serve the twofold purpose of recalling to mind the meditation and the resolution taken. St. Francis de Sales, in his *Introduction to the Devout Life*, particularly recommends meditation as a means of salvation.

Prayer

G UARDIAN of Jesus and Mary, unite my prayers with your fervent aspirations and holy contemplations. Each day I will place my resolutions under your protection and that of my mother Mary, and under this double safeguard I will rest in the full assurance of one day attaining to the sublime height gained by those who applied themselves with zeal and fervor to the constant practice of this holy exercise. Teach me, dear father, to unite my prayers with those of Jesus and Mary, and grant that, after imitating you closely here on earth, I may one day share in the joy and happiness of heaven. Amen.

Resolutions

1. During the course of the day, recall to mind the preceding reflections.
2. Learn to become habitually recollected.
3. Resolve to make a meditation every day.
4. Recite today, on your knees, Psalm 51, "Miserere."
5. Pray both the Our Father and Hail Mary once and "St. Joseph, pray for us" three times.

Aspiration

"St. Joseph, most persevering in prayer, pray for us."

Scripture Verse

"Rejoice always. Pray without ceasing." (1 Thessalonians 5:16-17)

Daily Meditation

"Let us consider how profound and tranquil must have been the life of St. Joseph, who, whether at work alone or with companions, had his heart and mind centered on God. We behold him ever the same; his noble and serene countenance bearing that indelible mark that the constant union of the soul with God always imprints. Here is our model. Let us endeavor, after his example, to acquire this interior recollection, which will enable us to overcome temptations, whatever be their nature or strength."

Editor's Note: The forms of habitual prayer that provide the means to interior recollection as discussed in today's meditation are reflected in the outline of prayer practices for each day of *The Month of St. Joseph.* Try to pray frequently throughout the day—each day—the aspiration provided, raising your heart in prayer. Follow through with the resolutions for each day, choosing perhaps the most fruitful one for your particular needs. In addition, devote some time daily to prayerfully reflect upon the consideration contained in the "Daily Meditation" section. If you are faithful to these practices throughout the month of March, you will be well on your way of establishing the habit of prayer that leads to a habitual interior recollection. Invoke the assistance of St. Joseph in these daily endeavors to acquire the virtue of interior recollection that he models.

Fifth Day
St. Joseph, Model of Justice

FIRST Point: St. Joseph was just. Every Christian should strive to merit the attribute of justice. It is not sufficient for him to possess honesty and uprightness. An honest man may be guided solely by the uncertain light of reason; and he may be governed by a conscience that is perhaps influenced by public opinion. The just man, on the contrary, is directed by the Word of God and by the will of God, as clearly demonstrated in the Church, and he relies on the assistance of grace for the accomplishment of the divine will in himself. He says with David, "Make me understand the way of your precepts, and I will meditate on your wondrous deeds. . . . I will run the way of your commands when you give me a docile heart" (Psalm 119:27 and 32).

These are beautiful words—the sense of which is a thousand times repeated by the prophet. St. Joseph must have pronounced them frequently, for they were ever in his heart. It was the law of God, the will of God, and the Word of God that served him as the rule, the principle, and the support of his life and actions. What is our principle, and what is our rule of action? Let us not be content with gaining the esteem of men, and being considered honest according to the standard of public opinion. As Christians and children of God, we should regulate our conduct by the example of Jesus Christ and the will of the Eternal Father.

Second Point: St. Joseph was just; justice, in the language of the early Church Fathers, embraces all virtues. By failing in one, we shall incur the displeasure of Him who instilled them all; for as St, James says, "For whoever keeps the whole law, but falls short in one particular, has

23

become guilty in respect to all of it" (James 2:10). St. Joseph was not governed by natural inclination nor self-interest. He was just—just always, in all things, and towards all persons. Can we render a like testimony of ourselves? Is there not some one virtue, the practice of which we entirely neglect? We frequently declare our natural bent of character as an excuse for the defects over which we should watch with the greatest care, on account of their having become to us a second nature. Alas! Character and habit cause us to commit many faults, and hinder us in the acquisition and practice of virtue.

Third Point: St. Joseph was just. The word "justice" reminds us that we owe God the fulfillment of every virtue, and it is in this sense that the word is used by the writers of the Sacred Scripture. To be just implies the possession of all virtues. God has an absolute right to our entire submission. He aids us by His grace in every act of supernatural virtue; hence our virtues and merits pertain much more to Him than to ourselves, on account of the powerful and indispensable assistance given us in the acquisition of them. St. Joseph, deeply impressed with these thoughts, was just and humble. We may say that he received innumerable graces, and was almost forced to respond to them; but every man is likewise given grace sufficient for his justification. Let us, then, be just. God will demand a rigorous account of the talents He has given, or rather confided, to each one of us. Every soul should increase in virtue according to the measure of graces which it receives. God, who is infinite justice, eternal bounty, and everlasting love, will be guided in His judgments equally by justice and mercy.

Prayer

ST. JOSEPH, intercede for us. Ten just souls would have sufficed to save the guilty city of Sodom. These ten souls could not have presented a homage as acceptable to God as you alone can offer Him. Their supplications could not have moved the Sacred Heart of Jesus as powerfully as you can awaken its compassion. Pray, then, for us, our kind protector, and save us from the divine anger. Obtain for us the grace to fulfill our duties, correct our faults, and practice virtue. Amen.

Resolutions
1. Recall frequently the preceding reflections.
2. Consciously practice justice in all your relationships, both business and personal.
3. Increase your awareness of those times you excuse yourself of your faults and shortcomings regarding the practice of virtue, especially justice.

Aspiration
"St. Joseph, model of justice, pray for us."

Scripture Verse
"Make me understand the way of your precepts, and I will meditate on your wondrous deeds." (Psalm 119:27)

Daily Meditation
"It was the law of God, the will of God, and the Word of God that served him [St. Joseph] as the rule, the principle, and the support of his life and actions. What is our principle, and what is our rule of action? Let us not be content with gaining the esteem of men, and being considered honest according to the standard of public opinion. As Christians and children of God, we should regulate our conduct by the example of Jesus Christ and the will of the Eternal Father."

Sixth Day
St. Joseph, Model of the Life of Faith

F AITH is the source, the rule, and the principle of the moral and spiritual life in the soul of the just man. His mind is impressed and occupied with the teachings and practices of faith. For the better understanding of this mysterious, all-ruling power, let us consider the life of faith in St. Joseph.

First Point: *Faith manifested in the life of St. Joseph —* St. Joseph submitted his understanding to the most profound mysteries of faith, even when these mysteries demanded the greatest sacrifices on his part. He believed that God spoke and manifested His will to him; hence his faith was reasonable. Our faith should be strong and lively, for it is eminently reasonable. We believe incomprehensible mysteries, it is true, but our belief is based on the Word of God, for He speaks by means of enlightened prophets and incontestable miracles. Ancient proofs, some of which are renewed in our own days, attest that the Church is the divinely authorized interpreter between God and man. Faith adds to the light of reason by manifesting new objects of knowledge, and it confirms truths of the natural order by its unexceptionable testimony. If the human intellect would gain in strength and power, let it be penetrated by the life of faith. The greatest and most sublime intellects were believers.

Second Point: *Life of faith in the heart of St. Joseph —* Faith assumes its true character and essential quality only in the heart of the believer. The damned believe and tremble. Their knowledge gives but remorse, and causes them to blaspheme the truths to which they are forced to testify. Such is not the faith of the just man; such was not the faith of St. Joseph. He revered the mysteries that were successively revealed to him, and he lived in the hope of the promised Redeemer, ardently desiring and awaiting His coming. Let us cherish our faith, and, above all, let the emotions of our heart be directed by its saving influence.

Every mystery of our holy religion proves the bounty and love of God towards His creatures. Faith finds a subject for thanks and love even in the contemplation of hell, into which the Devil gladly would drag us, that there we might join with him blaspheming God. Is not the fear of hell one of the most effective means to preserve us from the severity of the judgments of God? Though here on earth we may faintly perceive the greatness of the love that God bears us, it is only in heaven that we shall fully understand its plenitude.

Third Point: *Life of faith in the actions of St. Joseph* — In the various circumstances related in the Gospel concerning St. Joseph, we learn that he conducted himself according to the lights given him by God, and not merely to human wisdom and prudence. It is reasonable, therefore, to conclude that in those actions not mentioned St. Joseph was motivated by the same principle. He was a lover of justice, and he lived the life of faith. This life does not consist in the performance of great or singular actions, nor in certain religious practices, even though these practices should form a daily order of exercises. It is a series of acts ever active and always acting. Faith harmonizes the conduct and animates every work. It directs our thoughts and moderates and purifies our sentiments. It solicits the grace and blessing of God on our meals; it invokes his paternal care over our repose and our relaxations that they may exceed in nothing, and be conformed in all things to the Divine will. It supports, animates, and strengthens us in our labors and occupations, by teaching us to offer them to the majesty of God, or to honor His infinite bounty. It reminds us of heaven, and detaches us from earth, conformably to those words of St. Paul: "If then you were raised with Christ, seek what is above, where Christ is seated at the right hand of God. Think of what is above, not of what is on earth" (Colossians 3:1-2).

Prayer

M Y GOD, I firmly believe all the sacred truths the Catholic Church believes and teaches, because you have revealed them, who neither can deceive nor be deceived. Amen.

Resolutions

1. During the course of the day, recall to mind the preceding reflections.
2. Conform your will to the will of God.
3. Say a decade of the rosary for the souls in Purgatory.
4. Recite the Our Father and Hail Mary once and "St. Joseph, pray for us" three times.

Aspiration

"St. Joseph, model of the life of faith, pray for us."

Scripture Verse

"Think of what is above, not of what is on earth." (Colossians 3:2)

Daily Meditation

"He [St. Joseph] was a lover of justice, and he lived the life of faith. This life does not consist in the performance of great or singular actions, nor in certain religious practices, even though these practices should form a daily order of exercises. It is a series of acts ever active and always acting. Faith harmonizes the conduct and animates every work. It directs our thoughts and moderates and purifies our sentiments. It solicits the grace and blessing of God on our meals; it invokes His paternal care over our repose and our relaxations that they may exceed in nothing, and be conformed in all things to the Divine will. It supports, animates, and strengthens us in our labors and occupations, by teaching us to offer them to the majesty of God, or to honor His infinite bounty. It reminds us of heaven, and detaches us from earth."

Seventh Day
St. Joseph, Model for Christian Parents

FIRST **Point:** We find increased and perfected in St. Joseph that which we most admire in the patriarchs. The authority of the patriarch extends itself to all, and rules all things with a sovereign independence. The patriarch is a figure of God ruling his children and servants. He commands with an absolute authority that is always respected. St. Joseph appears thus to us in the family of which he is the head. Let us follow him to Bethlehem, to Egypt, and to Nazareth, and see him everywhere supremely exercising his paternal authority. He acts in the name of God, and as God's immediate representative. What family can be compared to this, where Jesus and Mary are members? What super eminent authority is implied in the power to command a God made man and His mother, the most privileged of all creatures; and at the same time, what admirable sweetness do we behold in the exercise of that patriarchal authority in him who is to become the type of Christian paternity!

Christian parents, in the government of your children, take for your model the patriarch St. Joseph. Learn from him to command according to the right you hold from God, and with the sweetness inspired by the example set by St. Joseph. Thus you will gain the obedience, respect, and love of your children. At the same time, understand that, to possess the authority of the patriarchs, it is necessary to have their spirit.

Second Point: Consider the spirit of the patriarchs. Holy Scripture tells us, "All these died in faith. They did not receive what had been promised but saw it and greeted it from afar and acknowledged themselves to be strangers and aliens on earth" (Hebrews 11:13). The greatest among them lived only in tents. Behold the spirit of the patriarchs! The passing enjoyments and terrestrial happiness that God allowed them did not divert their minds from the final object—the bliss of heaven; though faith taught them this could not be obtained until after the death of the God-Man and His triumphant Ascension into heaven. This spirit was perfected in St. Joseph. It is true he did not wait as long as his predecessors had waited for the accomplishment of these promises. The time of his death almost coincided with the era long and ardently desired by the patriarchs, when their souls should arrive at the possession of heavenly delights purchased for them through the merits of Jesus Christ. "The days of my pilgrimage are few and evil," said Jacob, [See Genesis 47:9, Douay-Rheims translation.] despite the many consolations with which divine Providence provided to ease his sorrows. Tradition tells us that the days of St. Joseph were fewer and more sorrowful. But the thought of heaven, which was to be the reward of his life of trials and sacrifice, moderated his pains—that heaven of which the society of Jesus and Mary had already given him a foretaste; that heaven which he greeted as near, was to him a subject abounding with desire, hope, and happiness.

Christian parents, such should be your spirit. "Here we have no lasting city" (Hebrews 13:14). Your children are given you more for the purpose of fitting them for heaven than of qualifying them for earthly positions. Possessing these thoughts and this spirit, a sense of your sublime duties will be imposed upon you, and impressed upon your children. Having the spirit of the patriarchs, you will possess their authority also, and thus perpetuate the patriarchal family.

Third Point: *The numerous posterity of the patriarchs* — The patriarchs numbered their children by families, and, from the tribute given for each member, they knew the number of their subjects. God multiplied them so that in number they equaled the sands of the sea or the stars of the sky. The family of St. Joseph is not less blessed in the prodigious number of his posterity. His is the family of Jesus and Mary—the Christian family. Who can enumerate this family, propagating its members everywhere, and with them their traditions and their faith? In what is the patriarchal family comparable to the children of St. Joseph? Thank God for having called you to be a member of this family, and prove yourself worthy of the favor by maintaining yourself and your family members in the spirit of Jesus Christ. Strive to merit for yourself a plenitude of the spiritual benedictions corresponding to the fruitfulness of the patriarchal family. Your counsels, authority, and example can engender numerous children to God and to the Church. How great is the posterity of the saints, multiplied in the orders of which they are the founders, in the sinners converted by their teachings, and the saints formed by their example, their writings, or their intercession!

Prayer

G LORIOUS St. Joseph, whom I am happy to call father since I belong to the family over which your patriarchal authority was exercised, obtain for me the grace to comply with my duties. In all my undertakings, obtain for me the spirit of detachment for created things, and a desire of heavenly gifts. Amen.

Resolutions

1. Recall to mind the preceding reflections.
2. Restrain your desire to converse on useless subjects.

3. Mortify your sense of taste at dinner.
4. Recite both the Our Father and Hail Mary once and "St. Joseph, pray for us" three times.

Aspiration

"St. Joseph, model for Christian parents, pray for us."

Scripture Verse

"We must consider how to rouse one another to love and good works." (Hebrews 10:24)

Daily Meditation

". . . take for your model the patriarch St. Joseph. Learn from him to command according to the right you hold from God, and with the sweetness inspired by the example set by St. Joseph."

Eighth Day
St. Joseph, Model of Remembrance of the Presence of God

FIRST Point: The patriarchs had a lively and a constant remembrance of the presence of God. This was due to the expectation and hope they had in their redemption by the Messiah whom God, in His boundless mercy, had promised them, and of which promise we have spoken in the preceding meditation. This remembrance was reinforced also by the frequent communications with which the Almighty favored them, either in dreams and illuminations, or by the ministry of angels. It was likewise due to the spirit of faith by which their love was animated. Their remembrance of the divine presence caused them to address Him with remarkable familiarity as the God of Abraham, of Isaac, and of Jacob. It was, at the same time, a powerful help to keep them in the practice of virtue, and make them advance in the perfect accomplishment of the divine will. "I am God the Almighty. Walk in my presence, and be blameless," said God Himself to Abraham (Genesis 17:1).

This attention to the presence of God is the ladder of perfection in every state and condition of life. St. Joseph, the last and greatest of the patriarchs, understood more clearly than did any other the excellence of this means of perfection, and he practiced it more faithfully. To convince one's self of this truth, it suffices to consider that St. Joseph was more impressed with heavenly thoughts than the angels could have been; that he was favored with intimate communications from God more frequently than they were;

and that his whole life was animated by faith. Other proofs are to be given, but, before we offer them, let us beg of God, through the intercession of St. Joseph, that our minds may be penetrated with an habitual sense of His presence, particularly during prayer and before our principal actions.

Second Point: Two things are necessary as a means of acquiring this remembrance of the presence of God in a direct and practical manner: First, to meditate on God and His perfections, and be impressed with the necessity and plenitude of His being. Secondly, it is necessary to remember that God, by His omniscience, knows fully and clearly the motives which animate our thoughts, words, and actions, and even the secret workings of our inmost soul. The mind and heart of St. Joseph, initiated as he was into the mysteries of the Incarnation and Redemption, must have been continually occupied with thoughts of God—His providence, His love for man, His omnipresence, and His other infinite attributes, all of which were revealed to St. Joseph. Manual labor did not distract his mind from the study of these truths. It occupied his time without debasing or entirely engaging his soul; on the contrary, his occupations left him even more liberty of thought and leisure than the study of science, politics, or the agitations of public life could have allowed him. Mechanics, laborers, and servants—all who are occupied in manual labor—can be interiorly united to God with much greater facility than can those whom they, perhaps, envy on account of belonging to a higher rank in life. Why do we not more frequently meditate on God, His perfections, and His love? Why do we not regard Him as a father, presiding over our labors, encouraging us by His presence and promise of the reward assured to those who offer and perform their works with the intention of pleasing Him?

Third Point: St. Joseph had not only the remembrance of the presence of God to occupy his thoughts and rule his life; he had God really present before his eyes in the person of Jesus Christ. "And I saw, and I gave testimony that this is the Son of God," says St. John in the beginning of his Gospel. [See John 1:32-34.] St. Joseph was the first witness of this wonder, in order that to him might be applied what was of old said to Abraham: "I am God the Almighty. Walk in my presence, and be blameless" (Genesis 17:1). This actual divine presence was almost unknown to the patriarchs.

We Christians have reason to rejoice in the privilege of being able to study the life of Christ in the Gospel, and in receiving Him in the Holy Eucharist. We may, at every instant, find consolation in this sweet and divine presence, in which is a treasure of grace and heavenly benediction. Do we imitate St. Joseph in this regard?

Prayer

H OLY St. Joseph, had I lived with you, my heart could have been easily impressed with a sense of the presence of God by your example. Obtain for me the grace that my heart be animated by a lively faith, so that all things may speak to me of God and remind me of His presence. Amen.

Resolutions
1. During the course of the day, recall to mind the preceding reflections.
2. Do not contradict others nor criticize their actions.
3. Submit your will to the will of others.
4. Recite both the Our Father and Hail Mary once and "St. Joseph, pray for us" three times.

Aspiration
"St. Joseph, model of the remembrance of the presence of God, pray for us."

Scripture Verse
"I am God the Almighty. Walk in my presence, and be blameless." (Genesis 17:1)

Daily Meditation
"We Christians have reason to rejoice in the privilege of being able to study the life of Christ in the Gospel, and in receiving Him in the Holy Eucharist. We may, at every instant, find consolation in this sweet and divine presence, in which is a treasure of grace and heavenly benediction. Do we imitate St. Joseph in this regard?"

Ninth Day
St. Joseph, Confirmed in Grace

FIRST Point: St. Joseph is the Israelite descendant of Abraham, Isaac, and Jacob. All the blessings given to the first-born of the patriarchs were united in him; and they assumed a new character previously only understood with difficulty by even the holiest persons, and seldom known through experience. St. Joseph, in the obscurity of his humble life, was animated by the spirit of the new law that the example and teachings of St. John the Baptist were soon to preach to all Judea. The old law promised temporal prosperity and eternal bliss to the Israelites who would be faithful in its observance. The joys of the other life were to them remote consequences dependent upon the coming of the Redeemer. The reward of a hundredfold in the life to come, promised by Jesus Christ for the trials and sacrifices endured here for His sake, must have been without attraction previous to the teachings of Christianity, and until a practical knowledge had been obtained of the merits of a soul suffering in union with a crucified God and leading a life most opposed to the yearnings of nature.

St. Joseph was, after the Blessed Virgin Mary, the first to manifest in his life this transformation of the blessings of the old law. Circumcised in the flesh according to the Jewish rite, he was circumcised in his heart in the new spirit. His share of family inheritance during his existence on earth was poverty, exile, persecution, and the Beatitudes of the Gospel. Do we understand and appreciate the blessings of the new law of love? Have we tasted of the happiness purchased by them? Are we circumcised in heart so as to joyfully endure poverty and suffering, and find therein that holy, inexpressible, hidden sweetness promised by the infallible Word of Almighty God? Do we not, on the contrary, more often imagine that impure happiness that is experienced by those who are possessed of riches and enjoy worldly pleasures—that which no spirit is more opposed to the spirit of the Gospel?

Second Point: St. Joseph was the son of David, the descendant of princely ancestors, to whom the throne of Judah had been promised as an eternal benediction. He was nevertheless a workman, and lived in obscurity, without influence, and not receiving the honors that accompany rank, position, and fortune. But he possessed a noble heart, which placed him far above his humble condition; and, despising the grandeur of an earthly kingdom, he has for a home the heart of Jesus, which is the new favor and the true royalty promised to the Christian family, of which he is the most illustrious representative. The royal line of David seemed to have terminated in the person of Joseph; but, on the contrary, it reigns forever through Joseph and Mary, ennobled and transformed by their connections with Jesus Christ. And do we, who belong to this royal family, comprehend and esteem this sublime elevation? Are our hearts animated by sentiments of noble, generous, royal greatness—even though in a humble and lowly condition—or do we desire the honors and privileges of those above us in worldly standing? If divine Providence has blessed us with riches and honors, do we not prize them too highly, forgetting that the love of Jesus should be the highest ambition of a soul created to the image of God?

Third Point: St. Joseph was the last just man under the old law, favored by God with dreams of prophetic import. He was the first who enjoyed those intimate ecstatic revelations with which the saints were afterwards blessed.

He derived an abundance of precious graces from his constant relations with Mary and with Jesus Christ, the source and giver of all graces, and the mediator between God and man. St. Joseph was not elated by these many mysterious favors. He faithfully cooperated with them, thus meriting an increase of grace. We Christians receive frequent communications from heaven. What use do we make of them? Our guardian angels watch over and obtain innumerable favors for us; the Holy Spirit, by His sanctifying and inexhaustible love, is in close union with a soul faithful to His inspirations; and the sacraments, particularly the Holy Eucharist, place us in the most intimate relations with Jesus Christ.

Christians! Recognize your dignity; live in correspondence with these precious, superabundant, and divine blessings.

Prayer

GLORIOUS St. Joseph, obtain for us the grace to profit by these blessings in which we as Christians participate. We are of the priestly and royal race, and have received the most glorious privileges. But are we conscious of the favors bestowed on us, and do we esteem them according to their worth? St. Joseph, your greatness consisted in virtue. Obtain for us this virtue that we may not by a criminal abuse of grace render ourselves more guilty in the sight of God. Amen.

Resolutions

1. During the course of the day, recall to mind the preceding reflections.
2. Listen to others with attention and respect, and, if there is error in their words, excuse their intention.
3. Say frequently, "Your will be done."

4. Fast one day this week in honor of St. Joseph.
5. Recite both the Our Father and Hail Mary once and "St. Joseph, pray for us" three times.

Aspiration

"St. Joseph, confirmed in grace, pray for us."

Scripture Verse

". . . whatever is true, whatever is honorable, whatever is just, whatever is pure, whatever is lovely, whatever is gracious, if there is any excellence and if there is anything worthy of praise, think about these things." (Philippians 4:8)

Daily Meditation

"Are our hearts animated by sentiments of noble, generous, royal greatness—even though in a humble and lowly condition—or do we desire the honors and privileges of those above us in worldly standing? If divine Providence has blessed us with riches and honors, do we not prize them too highly, forgetting that the love of Jesus should be the highest ambition of a soul created to the image of God?"

Tenth Day
St. Joseph, Model of Union with Jesus Christ

FIRST **Point:** Union with Jesus Christ is the most perfect expression of faith, and at the same time is its characteristic principle. Spiritual life receives its vitality from Jesus Christ, and is more productive of virtue and abundant in good works as the union of the soul with Him becomes more intimate. ". . . without me you can do nothing," says our Savior (John 15:5). Without the aid of grace, man cannot entertain a good thought. St. Paul says: "And no one can say, 'Jesus is Lord', except by the holy Spirit" (1 Corinthians 12:3). Our Lord makes use of a familiar and striking comparison in order to make this text more clear to us. Speaking to His apostles, He says: "I am the vine, you are the branches. Whoever remains in me and I in him will bear much fruit, because without me you can do nothing" (John 15:5). Thus Jesus Christ continuously communicates His graces to us. A father of the Church, using another comparison, says that union with God is to the soul what air is to the lungs; for as we could not live a natural life without those successive inhalations which at short intervals cause the beating of our hearts, neither can our souls live the life of grace unless they receive spiritual nourishment from Jesus Christ. Let us live so as to be able to say with St. Paul, ". . . yet I live, no longer I, but Christ lives in me" (Galatians 2:20).

Second Point: All true Christians experience the mysterious effects of the supernatural life, although they are not always perceptible to us. To experience these effects, it suffices that our souls be in a state of grace, and that we

43

frequently invoke Jesus Christ, and offer our principal actions through Him to God the Father. The more frequently we think of Jesus Christ, the more often we invoke Him; the more we beg His grace—which inspires us to imitate His example and obey His precepts—the more will the supernatural life be perfected in us. We should be most unhappy had we not these simple and easy means of advancing in virtue, acquiring merit, and increasing our reward. In our days all men aspire to freedom. The greatest liberty is that given us by Jesus Christ in uniting us with Himself, and enabling us to live in a Christian manner; for this union frees us from the slavery of the world, the flesh, and the Devil. It gives us a mastery over our faults and our actions, and elevates us far above all that could debase or degrade our dignity as Christians.

Third Point: St. Joseph understood and practiced this indispensable virtue of a Christian life. This union with God was not unknown to the just men of the old law. The principle and nourishment of their virtues were drawn from a belief in the merits of a Redeemer, and consequently from their union with Him. But this mysterious union has taken a wondrous development since the coming of the Redeemer, and the perfect fulfillment of the prophecies that previously gave His history to the just men who were not to see Him. St. Joseph, with the Blessed Virgin, was the first to contemplate the model of all justice. He saw and praised Him, adored Him as his God, and loved Him as his son. Are our lives in union with that of Jesus Christ? Let us repeat these words, imposed on us as a dogma: Nothing without Jesus; on the contrary all things by Jesus, in Jesus, and with Jesus by Him as mediator of grace; with Him, our model and our strength; in Him, the sole object of the satisfaction of the Father.

Tenth Day

Prayer

HOLY St. Joseph, I dare not repeat the words of the apostle, "I live, no longer I, but Christ lives in me." Those words, which are the device of holy souls that love and practice union with Jesus Christ, I find impressed on your heart, and, perhaps, gathered from your lips. But, alas! I feel that I yet live in myself, in my own thoughts, in my predominant faults, in the love of riches, and in the susceptibilities of my nature. Help me, powerful saint, to live for Jesus, with Jesus, in Him, and by Him. Amen.

Resolutions
1. During the course of the day, recall to mind the preceding reflections.
2. Let your thoughts, words, and actions be in union with Jesus.
3. Conform your will to the will of God.
4. Rise promptly in the morning at a given hour.
5. Recite both the Our Father and Hail Mary once and "St. Joseph, pray for us" three times.

Aspiration
"St. Joseph, enriched with graces, pray for us."

Scripture Verse
"This is the way we may know that we are in union with him; whoever claims to abide in him ought to live [just] as he lived."(1 John 2:5b-6)

Daily Meditation
"St. Joseph, with the Blessed Virgin, was the first to contemplate the model of all justice. He saw and praised Him, adored Him as his God, and loved Him as his son. Are our lives in union with that of Jesus Christ?"

Feast Day Reminder: If you are interested in praying a novena to St. Joseph in preparation for his feast day on March 19, begin that novena today. There is a traditional novena prayer to St. Joseph that begins on page 139. The novena will end on the day before his feast day. On March 19, you may—if desired—pray the consecration prayer to St. Joseph found on page 133 or pray the ancient prayer in his honor from page 148. Alternatively, you may wish to wait and make your consecration at the end of his month of March.

Eleventh Day
St. Joseph, First Confessor of the New Law

FIRST **Point:** The title given to St. Joseph at the beginning of this meditation might cause confusion in the minds of the faithful unless fully explained. Holy Mother Church gives him this title, and honors him in her public office as first among her confessors. We say that he was the first confessor of the new law, because he was the first just man who died under the empire and sweet influence of the law of love. In styling a great number of saint confessors, the Church does not mean to signify that they were priests and exercised the ministry of confessor, but it has adopted this manner of expression in the same sense that we would say to confess the faith, to confess the Gospel, or more simply still, to confess Jesus Christ. Consequently, the word "confessor" should be well understood and sufficiently explained in the following point.

Second Point: To confess Jesus Christ is to acknowledge and prove that we are His disciples; to believe all the truths taught us by the Church in the name of Jesus Christ, and to practice His law as His ministers make it known to us. The resistance of the spirit against faith—and the flesh against the world and morality—exacts from the faithful a kind of martyrdom, and our confession derives its value from their interior violence and exterior combats. To confess Jesus Christ in a manner worthy the title of saint and confessor is to believe the truths taught by the Church with a

47

more lively and ardent faith than do the generality of the faithful; but especially to live according to the teaching of the Gospel with a devotion and perfection bordering on heroism. The holy confessor does not bind himself to follow the rigorous precepts of the Gospel, but he attaches himself to the observance of the counsels, and follows as closely as possible the divine Model, thus becoming in his turn an example to others. St. Joseph, then, confessed Jesus Christ in the manner indicated in this point of our meditation. He was the first after the Blessed Virgin to imitate Jesus Christ in a perfection until then unknown. He listened to Jesus Christ, and implicitly believed the truths received from the lips of Eternal Truth. He not only followed the rigorous precepts of the Gospel, but he moreover practiced everything taught by the counsels, thus arriving at the heroic martyrdom of natural inclinations, and meriting the name of confessor. What simplicity, yet what incomprehensibility, in the concise words made use of in the Gospel: He was a just man!

Third Point: It remains now for us to examine ourselves and see if we confess Jesus Christ, His spirit, and His Gospel. We can enter heaven without being canonized saints and confessors, or without forcing on ourselves the fulfillment of the evangelical counsels; but it is not possible for us to attain eternal bliss if we do not, in some degree, imitate the saints and advance in the path of perfection. Not to advance is to recede. By a non-correspondence with the grace of God, we expose ourselves to lose our souls. St. Paul, addressing the faithful, says: ". . . if you live according to the flesh, you will die, but if by the spirit you put to death the deeds of the body, you will live" (Romans 8:13). Do our lives correspond with the profession of confessors of Christ and of His Church?

Let us seriously examine our hearts, and correct in them what we may find opposed to the virtues of a true Christian. Let us thank God for having sustained us in the good we have accomplished, and humble ourselves for the non-conformity of our words and actions with our profession. May the words of our Savior be applied to us: "I tell you, everyone who acknowledges me before others the Son of Man will acknowledge before the angels of God" (Luke 12:8).

That is to say, Jesus will, on Judgment Day, recognize before the Father, as His disciple, anyone who during life will have recognized Jesus as his Master.

Prayer

ADMIRABLE saint! We have not up to now confessed Jesus Christ in spirit and in truth. Help us to correct all in our conduct, everything that is contradictory to our faith. Obtain for us the courage and strength necessary to fulfill our obligations as Christians and followers of Christ Crucified. Grant that we receive all as coming from God, center our hopes in Him, and be faithful to His grace. Amen.

Resolutions

1. During the course of the day, recall to your mind the preceding reflections.
2. Do not question others through curiosity.
3. Let all your projects be subordinate to the will of God, and in all your undertakings depend on Him.
4. During meals attend to the wants of those at the table with you.
5. Recite both the Our Father and Hail Mary once and "St. Joseph, pray for us" three times.

Aspiration

"St. Joseph, first confessor of the new law, pray for us."

Scripture Verse

"Everyone who acknowledges me before others the Son of Man will acknowledge before the angels of God." (Luke 12:8)

Daily Meditation

"It remains now for us to examine ourselves and see if we confess Jesus Christ, His spirit, and His Gospel. We can enter heaven without being canonized saints and confessors, or without forcing on ourselves the fulfillment of the evangelical counsels; but it is not possible for us to attain eternal bliss if we do not, in some degree, imitate the saints and advance in the path of perfection. Not to advance is to recede. By a non-correspondence with the grace of God, we expose ourselves to lose our souls."

Twelfth Day
St. Joseph, Model of Hope

FIRST Point: Christian hope is a virtue which has for its first object future and eternal life—that is to say, the possession, knowledge, and love of God during all eternity—and for its second object the graces necessary as a means of attaining this supreme end. Hence, it leads us to believe that our past sins have been forgiven, and that God will raise us up and have pity on us if we should have the misfortune again to fall into them, though at the same time making us entertain the sentiment that God in His mercy will give us grace to guard against new falls. Moreover, it hopes and incessantly prays for the signal favor of final perseverance. How sweet are these thoughts, and how consoling this obligation of confidence in the loving kindness of our heavenly Father towards His children!

Christianity alone makes hope a virtue, for it alone teaches us the opposite excesses of defiance and presumption. The unfortunate traitor Judas sinned against the virtue of hope by defiance and despair. To guard against presumption, we must rely on God alone, and distrust ourselves. Presumption caused St. Peter to deny his divine Master. Let us be penetrated with these thoughts, and dwell on them, and beg of God the virtue of hope through the intercession of St. Joseph, who practiced it in its perfection.

Second Point: The virtue of hope corresponds in a marvelous manner to the title of confessor, which, with Holy Mother Church, we gave to St. Joseph in yesterday's med-

itation. To all bearing this title, the Church applies this
device of Christian hope. Happy is he who has not placed
his hopes in the things of earth; and, indeed, this is one of
the most precise lessons given us by Jesus Christ, and one
that makes the difference between the old and the new
law. The expectation of the Jews looked forward to transi-
tory joys and terrestrial rewards. Jesus Christ entirely
erased from His law this hope allowable to the just men of
old. The inconstant happiness of earth must be subservient
to hope; and the true Christian will place no value on the
joys of this life, since his proposed goal is eternal joy with
God. The former teachings of Jesus Christ in the Beatitudes
are the points of introduction to His doctrine. All the confessors of the new law must have understood the lessons
and examples of Jesus Christ from this point of view, and
St. Joseph was the first to receive and follow them. May
the sentiments relative to Christian hope in this meditation affect our lives and actions, and tend to enkindle in
our hearts the same degree of this virtue to which St.
Joseph attained!

Third Point: Neither earthly joys nor human consolations mingled in the hope of St. Joseph. His future life on
earth and in heaven was blended in the one same hope and
love. Let us not view the condition in which Providence
placed him as a preventative against the reverses of fortune.
It was not to aid his great soul in the practice of humility
that Joseph was poor and lived in poverty, but it was to
teach us how our choice should be directed. Had he been
rich, he would have sacrificed all and despised the worldly
advantages of a brilliant future, in order to become more
closely attached to the hopes of eternal life, to follow the
example of our divine Master, and have impressed more
deeply on his mind and heart the desire of eternal life. Or

if, in obedience to the will of God, he had been obliged to live in prosperity, his whole life would have been characterized by voluntary self-denials, renunciation, and sacrifice. This is a valuable lesson, from which we must derive profit. We are not obliged to forego all pleasures and joys; but we should not allow our hearts to become attached to them, so that in the enjoyment of them we forget the desire of heaven. The more we seek for earthly happiness, the less we think of heaven; and the practice of hope, as taught in the first part of this meditation, would become impossible. "Let us reach out our hearts toward God in heaven!" (Lamentations 3:41)

Prayer

HOLY St. Joseph! Your name is linked with hope. Obtain for me this gift, and let my soul be impressed with its sweet and amiable obligation of hoping all things from God. Grant that I may never again place confidence in human support, nor my happiness in perishable goods. Let the thought of the judgments of God only awaken a new cause for love. Teach me to live as a Christian, and to become worthy of the hope that your soul so fully appreciated. May I confide in God as the author of my salvation, hoping all things from His mercy, desiring to possess Him, the source of true joy, despising all earthly goods, guarding against them by continual sacrifice, and preparing my soul for the delights of heaven. Amen.

Resolutions

1. During the course of the day, recall to mind the preceding reflections.
2. Address your inferiors attentively and politely.
3. Observe mortification of the eyes.
4. Recite both the Our Father and Hail Mary once and "St.

Joseph, pray for us" three times.

Aspiration
"St. Joseph, model of hope, pray for us."

Scripture Verse
"Let us reach out our hearts toward God in heaven!" (Lamentations 3:41)

Daily Meditation
"We are not obliged to forego all pleasures and joys; but we should not allow our hearts to become attached to them, so that in the enjoyment of them we forget the desire of heaven. The more we seek for earthly happiness, the less we think of heaven; and the practice of hope . . . would become impossible."

Thirteenth Day
St. Joseph, Model of Patience and Mortification

FIRST Point: The whole life of Jesus Christ was a cross and a martyrdom, says the author of *The Imitation of Christ*. We may say that the life of a Christian must be the same. This conclusion is drawn from the Gospel. It resumes the teaching of the Apostles and proves that suffering is the chief characteristic in the lives of the saints. On this principle, and following these models, we must reflect on the necessity of sufferings. Coming from God, we must make them meritorious by a voluntary acceptance and loving offering, and sometimes even impose them on ourselves by generous acts of mortification and sacrifice. We have learned that the Christian must be a confessor by confessing Jesus Christ and Him crucified. These acts of mortification—directly opposed to nature and painful to it—bear testimony of our love for Jesus. Thus the name of "Christian" may be regarded as synonymous with that of "martyr." This is a severe but important lesson, one which, if understood and practiced, would be a synopsis of all others, and which we seek, in the resolutions taken each day of this month, to implant in our souls, and to teach to others. St. Joseph is our model in this; we can apply to him in a true sense the beautiful and noble title of martyr.

Second Point: St. Joseph suffered in his senses, his mind, and his soul. First, we look at his senses. He was a poor workman, and this occupation must have been painful to him, since he could number kings and chiefs of nations among his ancestors. The journey to Bethlehem and the flight and sojourn in Egypt were the cause of inexpressible suffering to him. Second, in his mind he endured painful apprehensions and motives of fear, less for himself than on account of those two precious beings who were placed in his charge, and whom he had to support and protect. Without imagining unknown perils, he knew enough of the Incarnation and Redemption to be convinced that the Savior of the world would pay a great price for our ransom. His soul, as well as that of Mary, was pierced by the words of Simeon, and reflection often brought to his mind the mysteries in which he was an intimate participator. Thirdly, we examine how Joseph suffered in his soul. There was no martyrdom more painful than the suffering to which Almighty God was pleased to subject St. Joseph during the first periods of the Incarnation. God concealed the mystery from him and made him witness of the condition of the Holy Virgin, his chaste spouse—a condition which seemed to accuse her of infidelity towards him and towards God. Mary, our holy and sweet mother—Mary, the Virgin Immaculate—must herself have suffered in the mental anguish of St. Joseph. Then reciprocal anxiety must have increased in one the suffering of the other. Add to this suffering that which was caused by the three days' loss of Jesus, and again the repulses met at Bethlehem, probably in Egypt, and at Nazareth. Moreover, in this detail of the sufferings of St. Joseph, we have mentioned only those coming directly from the hands of Providence; other voluntary sacrifices and self-imposed mortifications are the secrets of heaven.

Third Point: We have explained the doctrine of self-denial, and given a great, touching example. Let us now compare our own conduct with this lesson and model. How far advanced are we in Christian mortification? Do we understand and practice its maxims, and do we comprehend its importance, its advantages, and its indispensable necessity, whether for the expiation of our sins, to prevent new relapses, or to advance in virtue—each act of which is naturally an effort or sacrifice—or to detach us from earth, and make the hope of heaven dearer and more precious to us—whether, in thought and in deed, to resemble Jesus Christ, who suffered so much for us, and thereby give Him the strongest proof of our tender affection?

The thought of testifying our love for God, and manifesting our gratitude for His benefits to us, and our happiness in being allowed to endure pains and sacrifices for Him in commemoration of the sufferings, sacrifices and offenses that He endured for us should incessantly incite and inspire us to bear patiently all the sufferings, pains and sacrifices in life. But, alas! Our most essential duties seem insupportable, for the manner in which we fulfill them indicates the repulsion we have for them. Let us be humbled at our weakness, and pray for more generosity.

Prayer

GLORIOUS St. Joseph, you were a martyr in imitation of the Blessed Virgin, your holy spouse, and the queen of martyrs. You, through prophetic revelation, have been on Calvary, and endured the lingering death of compassion, which in the Virgin Mother surpassed all the torments of martyrs. May you be blessed, our protector and father, for it was for us that you did suffer! But your soul, sustained by grace under the weight of its trials, was prepared by sufferings and voluntary sacrifices. Pray that I may be inspired to imitate your example. Amen.

Resolutions

1. During the course of the day, recall to mind the preceding reflections.

2. Make some sacrifices of your choosing after the spirit of St. Joseph.
3. Recite both the Our Father and Hail Mary once and "St. Joseph, pray for us" three times.

Aspiration

"St. Joseph, first imitator of the sufferings of Jesus Christ, pray for us."

Scripture Verse

". . . whoever does not take up his cross and follow after me is not worthy of me." (Matthew 10:38)

Daily Meditation

"How far advanced are we in Christian mortification? Do we understand and practice its maxims, and do we comprehend its importance, its advantages, and its indispensable necessity, whether for the expiation of our sins, to prevent new relapses, or to advance in virtue—each act of which is naturally an effort or sacrifice—or to detach us from earth, and make the hope of heaven dearer and more precious to us—whether, in thought and in deed, to resemble Jesus Christ, who suffered so much for us, and thereby give Him the strongest proof of our tender affection?"

Fourteenth Day
St. Joseph, Model of the Love of God and of Sufferings

FIRST **Point:** After the meditation made yesterday on the sufferings of St. Joseph, we must not imagine that our venerated and glorious protector had severe points of character, caused by sorrow and contracted by affliction. Calmness and mildness marked his whole demeanor, particularly his angelical countenance. Nevertheless, he at all times suffered intensely. The mystery of this mildness, peace, and even joy, amidst sufferings, is explained by the influence of the love of God on the endurance of suffering and crosses, and the reciprocal influence of the love of sufferings and crosses on the development in us of the love of God. The love of God! These few words explain better than all others the great doctrine of the necessity of mortification and sufferings. Let us examine the subject of yesterday's meditation still more closely, and, placing ourselves at the foot of the Cross, beg of St. Joseph that its sweet and precious influence may excite us to the love of suffering in union with Jesus.

Second Point: When we truly love God, we feel ourselves drawn to the practice of mortification and to the love of sufferings: First, because he counsels and commands them. He makes use of an express command, in which he places every one under the necessity of making sacrifices. "If anyone wishes to come after me, he must deny himself and take up his cross daily and follow me" (Luke 9:23). This is not simply an invitation, but a command, and one that is not addressed to a class of persons, but to all who desire to be Christians. We find in the Gospel several other maxims prescribed as this one, and numerous others that may be regarded as counsels. But counsels are sufficient for those who love. When love is sincere, it is easy to comply with the will of the beloved. Second, God was the first to endure sufferings for love of us. We have already alluded to this motive and would not again refer to it were it not so easy to repeat to ourselves, "Jesus Christ has loved me and delivered Himself to death for me." What a happiness for me to suffer for Him, like Simon of Cyrene, who assisted Him in carrying His Cross, and accompanied Him on His way to Calvary! Third, God would not have advised nor commanded sufferings, nor would He have given us an example of love of sufferings, were they not to be in turn the strongest and truest proofs of our love towards Him. God is spiritual. The most touching expression that can be used to testify our sentiments towards Him may be but formulas uttered by the lips without moving our hearts; but sufferings endured for God, and sacrifices and crosses offered to Him manifest more strikingly than words could that we love Him purely for Himself. This is proof of our love, the one, too, which God desires, as it is given by the heart, whose most sensitive and delicate fibers, often bleeding and torn in nature's conflict, are looked upon with infinite appreciation by our divine Jesus, who will Himself in heaven become our only love and consolation.

Third Point: The love of crosses and sufferings dilates our hearts and rapidly increases the love of God in them. Those who fear crosses naturally shrink from the exercise of the works of mercy, from the frequent reception of the Sacrament of Penance and Reconciliation, and the correction of their faults, whereas, the love of sufferings removes all obstacles which hinder, embarrass, and finally force us to desist entirely from the love of God. When the possession of earthly joys and benefits satisfies our hearts, we forget heaven; but when oppressed with sorrow and affliction, we instinctively draw nearer to God and have recourse to prayer. When all around becomes dark, and by providential concurrent circumstances or the heroism of our own will, we suffer in abandonment, then God becomes our resource, our support, and our hope; and the invocation, "O God, come to my assistance; O Lord, make haste to help me" (Psalm 70:1, Douay-Rheims translation) comes from the depths of our hearts. God manifests His love in a most tender and paternal manner towards those who generously suffer for him. This mercy of God removes the bitterness of sufferings without destroying it. The sting is felt, but the balm of divine consolation is immediately poured over to heal the wound. Thus suffering produces love, and love produces suffering in all souls, as well as the soul of St. Joseph, whose heart was ever animated with divine love. Let us believe this doctrine and imitate this model.

Prayer

HOLY St. Joseph, by our love for you and admiration of your spirit of the Cross, we beg of you to obtain that our sentiments may become like unto yours. You could exclaim with King David, "My heart is ready, O Lord! My heart is ready." Then shall my soul be prepared for the loving designs of Providence, who realizes spiritual progress only by sacrifices and denials. Amen.

Resolutions

1. Let your mind and heart be impressed with the truths mentioned in the two preceding meditations.
2. Desire a more ardent love of God and of the Cross.
3. Receive willingly and endure patiently all afflictions that God may send you.

4. Recite both the Our Father and Hail Mary once and "St. Joseph, pray for us" three times.

Aspiration

"St. Joseph, ardent lover of God, pray for us."

Scripture Verse

"O God, come to my assistance; O Lord, make haste to help me." (Psalm 70:1, Douay-Rheims translation)

Daily Meditation

"The most touching expression that can be used to testify our sentiments towards Him may be but formulas uttered by the lips without moving our hearts; but sufferings endured for God, and sacrifices and crosses offered to Him manifest more strikingly than words could that we love Him purely for Himself. This is proof of our love, the one, too, which God desires."

Fifteenth Day
St. Joseph, Model of Ardent Charity

C HARITY is the most excellent and renowned of all virtues, including all the others, and giving them their true value and perfection. It is the noblest exercise of our faculties. Its influence produces the principal and essential difference between Christian virtue and human morality. Its practice is on earth, but its perfection is only in heaven.

First Point: To love God seems simple and agreeable to the reasoning mind. God manifests Himself in the beauty, grandeur, and sublimity of His wondrous works. Nevertheless, it is a remarkable fact that, although we hear the Word of God discussed in beautiful and appropriate terms, we seldom or never see visible proofs of love towards Him. Natural strength and virtue are too weak to produce that act of supreme love that makes us prefer God above all things, and retain a deep and durable impression of love for Him; still it is not only possible, but easy, for a Christian to love God.

Besides the eternal works of God, which always inspire one with an idea of His infinite perfections, a Christian has the revelations of faith opening to his view a new field more vast—and a thousand times richer and more varied—from which shines forth the grandeur, beauty, and, above all, the goodness of God. Revelation is truly a field of mysteries, where all is splendor and beauty, greatness and sublimity; but let us repeat, more clear than anything else, goodness and love. Moreover, as it is only by grace that the Christian is enabled to love God with his whole heart and soul, mind and strength—in a word, as God deserves to be loved—so those who do not correspond to this grace do not love God as He should be loved.

Second Point: St. Joseph loved God with an ardent love. He was just; and perfect love of God and justice are inseparable. As he was extremely just, he loved the source of all justice to an extreme degree. Contemplating in their true light the grandeur and extent of the mysteries of Christianity, which are the most inspiring testimony of the incomprehensible works of God and of His infinite bounty, he was attached to them by the closest and most tender ties. These sentiments were elevated and consecrated by an abundance of celestial favors and graces, greater than which were given to none but the Blessed Virgin Mary. How sweet to contemplate St. Joseph, not before the tabernacle where dwells the God of love, not at the foot of the Cross where God died for us, but carrying in his arms, and near his heart, the God Incarnate, the Infant God of love, who wished to be called the Son of Joseph. We are allowed to become participators in this happiness of our glorious saint by loving God with our whole souls.

Third Point: Do we love God? Being Christians, we can and must love Him, and manifest our love by acts of love; saying our morning and evening prayers devoutly; loving Him above all things—that is to say, more than all the goods of the world, the interests of fortune, and more than anything created. We should love God with our whole hearts, not dividing our affections between the Creator and the creature, but loving all things in God and for Him, since our Lord Himself tells us that we cannot serve two masters. We should love God with all our strength, not sparing ourselves in anything when the accomplishment of the will of God is concerned. We should love Him as the saints loved Him, as St. Joseph loved Him, and as did a holy priest, the Curé of Ars, who, with sweet simplicity, said, "God created little birds to sing, and they sing; God created man to love Him, and he does not love Him."

Prayer

H OLY St. Joseph! My prayer today will be an act of love, which I will beg you to present to God. I desire to love God, His holiness and infinite power. I desire to love the Sovereign Bounty, Him who is love, and who loves me with an indescribable love. In Him I will place my consolation and my strength here on earth, and my hope of supreme bliss in heaven. Amen.

Resolutions

1. During the course of the day, recall to mind the preceding reflections.
2. Be diligent in the fulfillment of duty.
3. Sacrifice all affection for vain and trifling objects, and generously attach your hearts to the eternal welfare of your souls.
4. Do not listen to frivolous or uncharitable conversations.
5. Recite both the Our Father and Hail Mary once and "St. Joseph, pray for us" three times.

Aspiration

"St. Joseph, ardent lover of God, pray for us."

Scripture Verse

"You shall love the Lord, your God, with all your heart, with all your soul, and with all your mind." (Matthew 22:37)

Daily Meditation

"We should love God with our whole hearts, not dividing our affections between the Creator and the creature, but loving all things in God and for Him, since our Lord Himself tells us that we cannot serve two masters. We should love God with all our strength, not sparing ourselves in anything when the accomplishment of the will of God is concerned. We should love Him as the saints loved Him, as St. Joseph loved Him."

Sixteenth Day
St. Joseph, Head of the Holy Family

I N OUR days, revolutions are common. The spirit of
revolt could not originate in society. It must be produced to a certain degree by the habits formed in family
relations. In the family of Jesus, Mary, and Joseph we see
order, peace, and calm serenity ruling all things. There
neither talent nor merit claims the right of command; on
the contrary, the greatest in merit and dignity obeys the
least, and the will of God is the law of their lives. Let us
examine each member of the Holy Family, and learn our
duty from them.

First Point: *The Father* — He is the representative of
God, the head and director of the household; but St. Joseph
in this capacity exercises his authority with all simplicity,
humility, and sweetness. He is continually brought before
God by the weight of the double responsibility towards the
mother and the Child. Joseph was obedient to God in all
things. He is the model after which fathers should govern.
St. Paul warns them to avoid provoking impatience, anger,
or hatred by rough, harsh, irritable commands, or by the
severity of their punishments, which are allowable only to
repress disobedience or natural tendency to evil. Were the
hearts of all fathers animated with the love of Jesus and
of Mary, as was the heart of St. Joseph, their actions governed by the same principles, and their affections nourished by the same thoughts, their lives would close with
the same desires.

67

Second Point: *The Mother* — All that Mary saw and heard was treasured in her heart (See Luke 2:19.), so that she might impart it to others. She allowed herself to be governed by St. Joseph without remark or resistance, well knowing the motives by which he was inspired. Whenever she interposed her authority, it was done by way of supplication, as at Cana, or by a tender maternal reproach, as in the Temple. Silence, reserve, tears, and prayers should be the habitual resource of Christian mothers. A mother's sphere becomes extended when a father fails in his duty, compromises his authority, and even provokes resistance by his disorderly conduct. But we prefer to imagine ourselves in the heart of a Christian family, where the parents are all that God wishes them to be. A Catholic mother should imitate the Blessed Virgin in her prudence, reserve, and submission to the will of her husband; and the care of her children should be her chief duty. Though she exercises less authority over them than the father does, her influence is much greater than his. If mothers only knew the power of tears over the hearts of their children, and the value of prayers in their behalf with the Heart of Jesus, their lives would be offered as a continual sacrifice for the salvation of those entrusted to their care.

Third Point: *The Child* — Children should obey their parents. The only history of the childhood of Jesus given in the Gospel is, ". . . and [he] was obedient to them" (Luke 2:51). It adds, it is true, that He grew in grace before God and man; but this was a consequence of His submission and obedience. The virtue of obedience comprises all the others. Children that are submissive and obedient to God and their parents will also increase in virtue, grace, and merit before God and man. Once only did our Lord seem to resist, or at least offer an excuse to His parents; when they complained of His having fled from them for three days, He said, "Why were you looking for me? Did you not know that I must be in my Father's house?" (Luke 2:49). There is but one circumstance in which a child is authorized to act contrary to the wishes of his parents—that is when the glory of God and the salvation of his soul is concerned. He should then say, as did Jesus, "Do you not know that the interests of God, our Father in heaven, must first be considered, and that obedience to parents should be subordinate to the will of God?"

Prayer

GREAT St. Joseph, not to you alone do I this day address my prayer. I desire to invoke the whole family, of which you are the father. Holy and amiable family of Nazareth—Jesus, Mary, and Joseph—protect Christian families, particularly mine. Let humility, meekness, obedience, and all virtues dwell in it. May the members composing it be united in you, that death may not separate them. May those bearing the cherished names of father, mother, brother, sister, or friend meet in heaven. Amen.

Resolutions

1. During the course of the day, recall to your mind the preceding reflections.
2. Seek to learn from others rather than to teach.
3. Be obedient to parents and superiors.
4. Mortify the sense of hearing.
5. Recite both the Our Father and Hail Mary once and "St. Joseph, pray for us" three times.

Aspiration

"St. Joseph, head of the noblest and holiest family, pray for us."

Scripture Verse

"So be imitators of God, as beloved children, and live in love . . ." (Ephesians 5:1).

Daily Meditation

"The greatest in merit and dignity obeys the least, and the will of God is the law of their lives."

Seventeenth Day
St. Joseph, Model of the Hidden Life

THE hidden life is fast becoming unknown, and every day we see less of it. Oh, that devotion to St. Joseph might bring persons to the practice of this life! The first cause detrimental to a hidden life is the aversion entertained by children for the activity of parenthood, and the desire to withdraw them-selves from their parental protection.

First Point: Let us contemplate the Holy Family of Nazareth; behold Jesus choosing His father's trade. He was an artisan and the son of an artisan. See St. Joseph, foster-father of the Infant God become His instructor and His master—bringing Him up to labor, teaching Him his trade; and Jesus, as a testimony of affection and gratitude towards St. Joseph, rendering him and the Blessed Virgin all the assistance that a good son would give his parents. What a touching picture! Let us try to reproduce it in every family, by advising children to consult God in prayer on the choice of a profession and state of life, and teaching them that wages may be used to advantage in every condition of life. Have those over whom you exercise influence cultivate habits of industry, and, if possible, have the daughter to pursue her occupations under the vigilance of her mother, the son to aid his father, and all to dwell together, rendering mutual services, which should be the honor and joy of a Christian family.

Second Point: Family life is strengthened by a holy observance of the Sunday; that is to say, by refraining from

71

servile works, assisting at Mass in the parish church, and seeking such amusements and relaxations as tend to unite the family circle. Let us contemplate the Holy Family at Nazareth and draw from its example the confirmation of our opinion. In that admirable family, no other absence is sought but that commanded by the law. Notice the sorrow and regret shown by Mary and Joseph at Jerusalem for having lost the Child Jesus, though they could not have reproached themselves with negligence. See them together in the Temple, at public prayer, at work, and at relaxations from duty. There was not a second occasion for the Blessed Virgin to search for her divine Son, whom she once supposed to be taken from her tender care. Christian parents and children, keep holy the Sabbath day! It is, by excellence, the day of the Lord; but it is also the day of rest for families. Remain in your own parish, let your recreations be holy, and taken as much as possible in common. O Christian parents! Have you not often cause to search, weeping and sorrowful, for your children? The Blessed Virgin Mary and St. Joseph had no cause for anxiety concerning the soul of Jesus; but you, alas! On those days and evenings, when your children spend hours from home, have cause for anxious search in fear; for it is not the mortal life that is in danger, but the immortal souls of your precious charges.

Third Point: Family ties are strengthened and affection nourished by the mutual interchange of thought, duties of respect towards the head of a family, instructions given to children, and the thousand other acts tending to attract the heart. Picture to yourselves the interior of the Holy Family at Nazareth. See Jesus, Mary, and Joseph at their meals, at work, and in conversation. What heavenly peace and complete happiness, by the presence and union of the father, the mother, and the Child! Ah, could all families spend more time together at home and find there the rest and pleasure sought for elsewhere; how much happiness would be obtained for the thousand desolate homes whose members—carried away by love of indulgence and forbidden pleasures—bring sorrow and misery to their families!

Prayer

HOLY St. Joseph! On this your feast day, make us enter in spirit into the house of Nazareth, honored by so many mysteries, but especially by the hidden life you led there for many years with Jesus and Mary. Obtain for us from the hearts of Jesus and Mary an esteem for a hidden life and the desire of practicing it after their example, with the interior virtues necessary for so holy an enterprise. Amen.

Resolutions

1. During the course of the day, recall to mind the preceding reflections.
2. Conform your will to the will of others.
3. Sacrifice personal tastes to the pleasure of others.
4. Seek the good of others at the cost of your own inclinations.
5. Recite both the Our Father and Hail Mary once and "St. Joseph, pray for us" three times.

Aspiration

"St. Joseph, model of the hidden life, pray for us."

Scripture Verse

"Remember to keep holy the sabbath day. Six days you may labor and do all your work, but the seventh day is the sabbath of the LORD, your God. No work may be done then either by you, or your son or daughter . . ." (Exodus 20:8-10).

Daily Meditation

"Family life is strengthened by a holy observance of the Sunday; that is to say, by refraining from servile works, assisting at Mass in the parish church, and seeking such amusements and relaxations as tend to unite the family circle." [**Editor's Note:** How much easier would the holiness of the hidden life be if this one precept alone were followed?]

Eighteenth Day
St. Joseph, Model of Artisans and Workmen

FIRST **Point:** Jesus and Joseph were artisans. Divine Providence selected this condition of life for them in order to honor and sanctify manual labor, which the nations of antiquity regarded as mean and debasing. Joseph and Jesus are in this capacity presented as models to those who earn their bread by the sweat of their brow. Laborers and mechanics participate more fully in the blessings promised to the poor in the Gospel than do those in more elevated positions, for they have less to fear from the curse that falls on the abuse of riches. True, their condition is in itself painful and unpleasant to nature, particularly at times when work fails or salaries decrease so as not to meet the demands of maintenance; yet in those trials they ought to be encouraged and consoled by the example of these great models, Joseph and Jesus. Let them choose St. Joseph for their patron and protector. Jesus, our divine Savior, gave up the employment of a carpenter during the last three years of His life in order to attend to His divine mission; but St. Joseph continued his labors until his death, and he was known among his contemporaries as "Joseph the carpenter."

Second Point: The duties of a laborer or mechanic are order and regularity in his habits of life, strict honesty in his commercial relations, a detestation of the use of false weights and measures and of deception in any form. Joseph was an honest and noble carpenter, or, in the widest acceptance of the expression, was just by excellence. Admire the sublime elevation of soul manifested in this holy descendant of Judah's kings. When we see him labor with his hands for maintenance, we perceive the nobility of character, purity of conscience, and delicacy of sentiment exhibited in the self-sacrificing spirit of the spouse of the most pure Virgin. What admirable simplicity is portrayed in his obedience to king and the laws of his country, even at the risk of excessive fatigue to the Blessed Virgin, who bore the Son of God in her most chaste womb.

Third Point: The secret of this ennobling and sanctifying influence on the actions of St. Joseph, even in his obscure condition, is the purity of intention that directed his every work. It is well known that the virtues of the Blessed Virgin and of St. Joseph were not made less brilliant by the obscurity of their lives; for in the sight of God, the Supreme and Eternal Truth, Mary and Joseph were higher than the greatest sovereigns. Self-love suffices to obscure the most meritorious and brightest act; and though the hidden virtues are less liable to be fashioned by the fatal illusions of self-love, still they are not entirely safe from its harmful influence, unless we keep constant watch over the movements of our hearts.

We must strive to acquire the habit of virtue, so that the good may predominate in us. Our actions become more meritorious—and the virtuous habits acquired more elevated—as our intention becomes centered in God. Of all the supernatural motives, that of charity is most capable of inciting our souls to good. We should offer to God every act, however insignificant, and let love for Him permeate every thought, word, and action. The poor and lowly can become great in merit and virtue, as did St. Joseph. They can imitate him as their model, and invoke him as their protector.

Prayer

HOLY St. Joseph, be the protector and model of all those who are obliged to labor for the support of their families. Teach them to fulfill their duties in a Christian manner; recall to their minds in what true greatness consists; and obtain for them fidelity to your example. May they learn from you that the secret of true happiness, even here on earth, is moderation of desires, patience, resignation, the hope of heaven, and the joy of loving and serving God. Amen.

Resolutions

1. Avoid all conversations having a tendency to make you dissatisfied with your condition in life.
2. Let the poor and lowly thank God for having called them to a state of poverty and those favored with wealth and luxury beg of God to enable them to use these gifts for their eternal salvation.
3. Recite both the Our Father and Hail Mary once and "St. Joseph, pray for us" three times.

Aspiration

"St. Joseph, model of artisans and workmen, pray for us."

Scripture Verse

"Blessed are the poor in spirit, for theirs is the kingdom of heaven." (Matthew 5:3)

Daily Meditation

"We must strive to acquire the habit of virtue, so that the good may predominate in us. Our actions become more meritorious—and the virtuous habits acquired more elevated—as our intention becomes centered in God. Of all the supernatural motives, that of charity is most capable of inciting our souls to good. We should offer to God every act, however insignificant, and let love for Him permeate every thought, word, and action. The poor and lowly can become great in merit and virtue, as did St. Joseph. They can imitate him as their model, and invoke him as their protector."

Nineteenth Day
St. Joseph, Model of Charity towards Our Neighbor

W E WILL now consider St. Joseph—especially today on his feast day—in his relations with his neighbor. As a carpenter, a voluntary exile, and a citizen of his native country, he proves to us—by his example—that of all the duties we owe to our neighbor, charity is the first.

First Point: The law of charity binds us equally towards God and our neighbor. It might be deemed necessary to use a different term by which to designate the supreme and absolute love we have for God in distinction from that we bear towards our neighbor. But to separate the love of God from the love of our neighbor would be to deny the nature of love which engages the dearest and most intense affections of the heart, and which disposes us to forget and sacrifice ourselves for those we love. The second commandment is like the first, says our Savior, so much so that its origin and its end are the same, for it is the image, the will, the love of God; in a word, it is God whom we love in our neighbor. We cannot separate the love of God and the love of our neighbor, for loving our neighbor in a Christian manner is loving God. "You shall love the Lord, your God, with all your heart, with all your soul, and with all your mind. . . . You shall love your neighbor as yourself" (Matthew 22:37 and 39). This precept is the expressed command of our Savior—strictly recommended to us—and its fulfillment will be the badge by which the disciples of Jesus Christ will be known. The heart of St. Joseph was inspired with this tender and devoted love for the whole human family.

Second Point: We must practice charity in our relations with our friends and enemies. It seems unnecessary for us to mention the duty of love for friends. Our Lord says, "For if you love those who love you, what recompense will you have? Do not the tax collectors do the same?" (Matthew 5:46). It is precisely that your friendship may not be similar to that of the unbelievers that your affecttions, thoughts, and hearts are referred to the example of St. Joseph. In his humble condition, his friends were few. None are mentioned in the Gospel, unless that title may be given to the shepherds and wise men who came to Bethlehem. Friendships that are produced by love of pleasure, sympathy of character, business relations, or natural affection independent of a higher and holier aim have not love of God for their motive. The Gospel, moreover, commands us not only to forgive our enemies and pray for them, but also to love them. This precept is violated by a great number of Christians. We demonstrate a cold reserve and resentment towards those who have offended or injured us; yet each day we say, "Forgive us our trespasses as we forgive those who trespass against us." These words should be dwelt upon until we are well impressed with their import.

Third Point: We owe the duty of charity towards all mankind. St. Joseph greeted his neighbor with a friendly smile, evoked by love; and as no one was excluded from the love of Jesus, neither did St. Joseph deny his love to anyone. Wherever Providence placed him, all displayed indifference towards him on account of his poverty; but he in return regarded them with affection, and desired their salvation. Let us strive to benefit someone each day of our lives, either by prayers or example, being particularly kind to those who offend us or demonstrate ingratitude towards us; and let us be convinced that Jesus Christ and His love are sufficient for us.

Prayer

G LORIOUS St. Joseph, your name is synonymous with sweetness and charity. Each word of the Gospel concerning you seems to exhale the perfume of these amiable virtues. Pray for us that we may imitate you in the avoidance of discontent, impatience, jealousy, hatred, bitterness, violence, and resentment, and obtain that our whole lives be animated by charity, that at death we may be received with mercy and love by the God of love. Amen.

Resolutions

1. Prepare to receive Holy Communion on this feast of St. Joseph.
2. Rejoice in the good of others.
3. Pardon all injuries.
4. Recite both the Our Father and Hail Mary once and "St. Joseph, pray for us" three times.

Aspiration

"St. Joseph, loving to all, pray for us."

Scripture Verse

"You shall love your neighbor as yourself." (Matthew 22:39)

Daily Meditation

"Let us strive to benefit someone each day of our lives, either by prayers or example, being particularly kind to those who offend us or demonstrate ingratitude towards us; and let us be convinced that Jesus Christ and His love are sufficient for us."

Twentieth Day
St. Joseph, Model of Humility

FIRST Point: The principal virtue in our relations with our neighbor is humility. This virtue, so little known among those absorbed by worldly pursuits and pleasures, is of purely Christian origin. We will speak here of a few of its characteristic traits. Humility is the submission of the mind and heart to the knowledge of our own misery and nothingness. Whatever increases and strengthens this knowledge may serve in some measure to develop one or more of the qualities of humility. In the first place, frequent reflection on the infinite greatness of God contributes much to this virtue, placing before our minds the contrast that naturally arises from the thought of His infinite perfections and our own unworthiness. We are but creature holding all we have from God. "What do you possess that you have not received? But if you have received it, why are you boasting as if you did not receive it?" says St. Paul in 1 Corinthians 4:7. This reflection serves to maintain in us sentiments of the most profound humility. We have, perhaps, offended God grievously; and in consequence of the inclination to evil that we find in ourselves, in spite of all our resolutions, we still continue to fall into many faults. "The just man falls seven times . . ." says the wise man in Proverbs 24:16.

We can of ourselves do nothing towards our eternal salvation—not even form a good thought—without the aid of that all powerful Being who created us. God must aid and support us in the accomplishment of all the good we do and yet how have we corresponded to this grace? Here are motives on which we can and must rely, particularly on the last, in order to be convinced of our spiritual misery. However, to have humility, it is not sufficient to submit with the mind alone to the knowledge just mentioned; for that of the heart is also necessary, inasmuch as we must not revolt or complain, but submit and be resigned, and even go so far as to desire to be perfectly well known and treated as we deserve. This is the sense conveyed in the expression of our Savior, ". . . learn from me, for I am meek and humble of heart . . ." (Matthew 11:29). This divine lesson, so difficult on account of the innate pride in us, we also receive, and should learn, from St. Joseph, who obtained it from the loving heart of Jesus, and we should earnestly implore Him to impart the secret of acquiring it to us.

Second Point: We have said that after charity, humility—more than all the other virtues—enables us to regulate our conduct towards our neighbor. The words of our divine Savior already quoted will make this more clearly understood: ". . . learn from me, for I am meek and humble of heart; and you will find rest for yourselves" (Matthew 11: 29). The word "meek"—used by Jesus before that of "humble"—and the words terminating the quotation reveal to us, in all its beauty, the doctrine we are to explain. Meekness—that virtue which of itself affords inexpressible delight—accompanied by the promise of so great a reward seems to be, by excellence, the virtue most needed for the gaining of our neighbor. Has not our Lord Himself said, "Blessed are the meek, for they will inherit the land" (Matthew 5:5); or, in other words, blessed are the meek, for they shall possess the heart of man? Meekness, says St. Francis de Sales, is the sister or flower of charity; but, mark well, we cannot be meek or even good Christians unless we are humble, and we will certainly be meek if we are humble of heart.

Humility then, such as we have characterized in the first point, must necessarily be accompanied by meekness. Have we understood it thus, and endeavored to make this our constant practice and the rule of our conduct towards our neighbor? Does our humility tend to bring him joy, calm, and peace? Does it afford rest to our own souls?

Third Point: This examination of ourselves is painful, because it is humiliating; and perhaps we are not yet sufficiently humble to undergo it as we should. Let us rest our minds and hearts in beholding a touching model of humility! Let us contemplate St. Joseph in the different conditions in which he was placed by divine Providence, and see his lowly humility! Not a word of complaint ever escaped him; no regret for the departed grandeur of his family; no thought of complacency on the mission fulfilled by him; he considers himself only as the servant and dispenser of the things confided to him. He conforms in all things to the divine will, never murmuring under the many crosses placed upon him. Meek and forbearing towards all, in humility he possessed his soul. Here is your model. In what do you resemble him? Implore his assistance in overcoming your many defects.

Prayer

O DEAR St. Joseph! Grant that by your example and that of my divine Savior I may become meek and humble of heart. You, who in this were a faithful imitator of Jesus, cause these virtues to enter deeply into my soul, and grant that by the practice of them I may become more and more like you. I abandon myself to you, and invoke your aid. This lesson of humility is one of the most difficult in the Gospel, but nothing is impossible to God. And you will be for me an all-powerful suppliant at the throne of grace, where my soul may be imbued with meekness and humility. Amen.

Resolutions

1. During the course of the day, recall to mind the preceding reflections.
2. Convince yourself of your miseries by reflecting on the goodness of God and your ingratitude.
3. Willingly accept the humiliations that may befall you.
4. Recite both the Our Father and Hail Mary once and "St. Joseph, pray for us" three times

Aspiration

"St. Joseph, meek and humble, pray for us."

Scripture Verse

"What do you possess that you have not received? But if you have received it, why are you boasting as if you did not receive it?" (1 Corinthians 4:7)

Daily Meditation

"Humility then, such as we have characterized in the first point, must necessarily be accompanied by meekness. Have we understood it thus, and endeavored to make this our constant practice and the rule of our conduct towards our neighbor? Does our humility tend to bring him joy, calm, and peace? Does it afford rest to our own souls?"

Twenty-First Day
St. Joseph, Model of Religious

FIRST Point: A religious vows the practice of the evangelical counsels by subjecting himself in a particular manner to perfect obedience. The Gospel does not tell us that St. Joseph contracted any such commitments, but we infer from tradition that he made a vow of chastity. Whatever may have been the nature of the promises by which he bound himself to God, the perfection of his life gives him a close resemblance to religious, and he is proposed to them as a model. A religious makes the three vows of poverty, chastity, and obedience. St. Joseph was poor, chaste, and obedient; but, at the same time, his manner and condition of life give him as a model to persons living in the world, and who wish to serve God more perfectly than the generality of Christians.

You who have made sacred commitments with God, renew them now with special fervor, and place them under the protection of St. Joseph. You who feel in your hearts the desire to lead a more perfect life by applying yourselves to the realization of the virtues, invoke your father, St. Joseph, for you are of his family. And you who live the ordinary lives of Christians, and do not feel yourselves called to the practice of the counsels, be faithful in fulfilling all the commandments required of you; for in this way progress will be gained each day, and at last a relative perfection will be attained. Not to advance is to recede. Place yourselves today under St. Joseph's protection and his holy prayers will serve as support to yours.

The Month of St. Joseph

Second Point: No religious by the fulfillment of his vows has ever attained so high a degree of perfection as St. Joseph. Living in the world, surrounded by the objects from which a religious separates himself—and even possessing them—reserving rights that the religious renounces, St. Joseph, by a continual self-denial and entire abandonment to the will of God, practiced the three virtues of poverty; chastity, and obedience in all that was in them most difficult, pure, and elevated. He was, it is true, proprietor of his little home and his working tools, but his was an ownership detached from all things, willing to be in exile, and ready to move wherever and whenever God desired him. St. Joseph was a husband, and he lived with his chaste spouse as her guardian, consoler, protector, and support. But he was the virginal spouse of the most pure Virgin. He commanded because he was the head of a family, the care of which was given him; and though he held the authority until his last breath, he nevertheless was most obedient, since he conformed himself to all the orders of Providence, and accomplished them with precision and eagerness, as is testified by the words of the Gospel. Let us imitate this beautiful model.

Third Point: In order to understand the degree of religious perfection attained by St. Joseph, we must consider that he was not sustained by any of those human motives that faith may stand for, though they be detrimental to perfection, since they afford natural pleasure. His life was hidden and unknown. He cared not for fame, nor for friendly encouragement, nor human patronage. The joy of a good conscience, the satisfaction of having fulfilled his duty, and the love of God were sufficient for him. In this he is a model for religious and all persons engaged by vow to the service of God. Let us examine the motive by which we are animated. If it be solely with a view of pleasing God and testifying our love for Him, let us thank God for giving us the grace to act thus. Let us not allow human motives to influence nor detract from vows so noble, pure, and sacred that we offer to God in testimony of our love for Him; and those in the world who live without having made any formal commitment binding them to the practice of the counsels and perfection should know that St. Joseph occupied a position similar to theirs, and that—although he made no religious vow—he was nevertheless more perfect than they are. Imitate him by daily aspiring to a closer union with Jesus Christ and fidelity to the inspirations of conscience.

Prayer

O BLESSED Joseph! Since Jesus while on earth was subject to you, rendered prompt obedience to your commands, and cherished you with a most special love and honor, how shall He now refuse you anything in heaven, where all your merits receive their full reward? Pray for me, therefore, holy patriarch, and obtain for me these necessary graces: first of all, that I may have a sincere contrition for my sins; that I may ever hate and fear all that is evil, and flee from it with firmness and constancy, especially from my most troubling sins: grant that I may amend my life daily more and more, and constantly apply myself to the acquiring of virtue, especially those virtues I need most; and that I may be kept safe amid the various temptations and occasions by which my soul may be exposed to the peril of damnation. For these and for all other needful graces, O holy Joseph, I commend myself to the goodness and mercy of my God, and to your fatherly care and intercession! Amen.

Resolutions

1. During the course of the day, recall to mind the preceding reflections.
2. Do not regard stubbornness and obstinacy as dignity of character; but let sincerity and goodness—or rather humility and meekness—be the true dignity you strive to attain.
3. Make some sacrifice that will enable you to lay aside an alms for the Holy Father.
4. Recite both an Our Father and Hail Mary once and "St. Joseph, pray for us" three times.

Aspiration

"St. Joseph, just and perfect man, pray for us."

Scripture Verse

"So be perfect, just as your heavenly Father is perfect." (Matthew 5:48)

Daily Meditation

"Not to advance [in the spiritual life] is to recede."

Twenty-Second Day
St. Joseph, Model of Obedience

FIRST Point: *The necessity of obedience* — Every man is obliged to obey. Every Christian should render implicit obedience to the commands of God and of His Church. We have previously considered the duty of children to obey their parents; we will now consider the obligation of obedience that binds us all. To obey is incumbent on all men. Though God does not Himself confer with us, nor send special messengers to us, as He did to Joseph, nevertheless He gives us His law, and manifests Himself to us through His Church in the teaching of His ministers; therefore the fulfilling of our duties is but an act of obedience. Moreover, all are, in a measure, dependent on certain authorties, and, be these civil, religious, or parental, we are bound in justice to render obedience to them. We obey God when we submit to lawful authority; on the contrary, when we refuse to obey those whom the will of God has placed over us, we disobey God Himself. St. Joseph obeyed the mandate of the Emperor Augustus in going to Bethlehem; but he had in view an authority far superior to that of a worldly prince, for he recognized the will of God in the command of his earthly ruler.

Second Point: *Advantages of obedience* — Scripture says, "An obedient man shall speak of victory" (Proverbs 21:28b, Douay-Rheims translation). In fact, the victory gained over self-love and pride in rendering obedience to others, and submitting our will to theirs, immeasurably multiplies the triumphs of a Christian, and these triumphs may be gained each day. According to another passage found in Scripture, "Obedience is better than sacrifice" (1

Samuel 15:22b). In explanation of this text, St. Gregory says in the sacrifice of victims, it is the flesh of animals that is offered to God; whereas, by obedience we sacrifice ourselves. The merit of one act of obedience may be extended to a series of acts and serve to consecrate them all to God; sometimes one act devotes an entire life to God. Thus St. Joseph, by obeying the orders of the emperor, procured the fulfillment of all the prophecies concerning the birth of our Savior. By his flight into Egypt, he consecrated several years of his life to the accomplishment of the designs of God. We should be grateful to God for giving us a means to acknowledge our desire of submitting to His will in the prayer He taught His disciples, "your will be done, on earth as in heaven" (Matthew 6:10). We should say these words with a lively feeling of our dependence on Him.

Third Point: *Qualities of Obedience* — St. Joseph obeyed in spirit and in truth. He followed the dictates of his conscience in the sight of God, and with the desire of pleasing Him; not caring how men should regard him, nor had he any fear of creating their displeasure, nor the desire of attracting their attention and admiration. St. Joseph obeyed promptly. The Scripture assures us that he executed the orders of God at the instant that they were made clear to him. What homage and love we may render to God by this ready obedience, and what a source of grace is opened for us if we submit promptly to the will of those authorized by our heavenly Father to command us! Love was the motive and principle of the obedience of Joseph. Where love is, obedience is sweet. All who are lawfully placed in authority hold their position by the will of God; and even though they be harsh, severe, pessimistic, and unkind, still they should be obeyed, on the consideration that God wills us to be subject to them, and thereby prove our love for Him.

Prayer

HOLY St. Joseph, obtain for me the true spirit of obedience. Help me to subdue my pride and submit my will freely to the most beneficial yoke of obedience. Let my soul be animated by humility like that of our mother Mary when she said: "Behold the handmaid of the Lord; be it done unto me according to Your word." Pray that I may understand the advantages and necessity of faithful obedience. Amen.

Resolutions

1. During the course of the day. recall to mind the preceding reflections.
2. Conform your will to the will of your superiors.
3. Render a prompt and loving obedience to those who command you.
4. Recite both the Our Father and Hail Mary once, and "St. Joseph, pray for us" three times.

Aspiration

"St. Joseph, most obedient, pray for us."

Scripture Verse

"Obedience is better than sacrifice." (1 Samuel 15:22b)

Daily Meditation

"St. Joseph obeyed in spirit and in truth. He followed the dictates of his conscience in the sight of God, and with the desire of pleasing Him; not caring how men should regard him, nor had he any fear of creating their displeasure, nor the desire of attracting their attention and admiration."

Twenty-Third Day
St. Joseph, Model of Obedience for Those in Authority

OBEDIENCE is a virtue that imparts peace to the faithful soul, religious or secular. Priests and religious are indeed happy in the certainty of always performing the will of God by obeying their rules and superiors.

First Point: *Obedience practiced by superiors and parents* —Religious superiors, as well as parents, have some higher authority to whom they owe subjection. Even the princes of the earth have superiors in those who direct them in either spiritual or temporal matters. It is a relief for those who command to feel that they are dependent on someone, whom they are to obey. To go still further, they can practice this virtue not only by obeying their superiors, equals, and the Church, but also in the manner in which they treat their inferiors or children, by listening with kind attention to them, and never making them feel their inferiority. Jesus Christ Himself teaches this in His conduct towards St. Joseph, and the life of this holy patriarch presents many examples of this admirable virtue.

Second Point: Superiors and parents, when commanding, should seek only the greater glory of God. With this disposition of mind and this intention in view, they will find that in commanding others they are invariably obeying God. The faithful practice of these two principles will give the command a mildness and force that it would not otherwise possess. Let us contemplate St. Joseph as superior in his domestic capacity over Jesus and Mary, and admire his sweetness and humility. This is our model. Do we resemble him?

Third Point: Parents and superiors—in fact, all who are placed over others—should have specified rules for the regulation of their different actions and exercises of each day. Thus, in the morning, they should strive to foresee all that may happen before evening, and thereby prevent many faults of inadvertence. Besides, by having a specified time for each action, they will have frequent occasion of exercising their fidelity in the practice of obedience. Again, contemplate St. Joseph in the cottage at Nazareth, dwelling with Jesus and Mary. Order and regularity attend his every action. He has a specified time for rising, for prayer, for meals, work, relaxation, and even for repose. The Gospel, telling of their journey to Jerusalem, says: "and when he was twelve years old, they went up according to festival custom" (Luke 2:42). From this, we may infer that all their actions were regulated according to rule.

Prayer

ST. JOSEPH, admirable model of obedience, teach me to obey as you did; grant that, in commanding others, I myself may not lose the spirit of obedience. Assist me, I beseech you, dear saint, and with your aid I will be sure of success. Amen.

Resolutions

1. During the course of the day, recall to mind the preceding reflections.
2. Accustom your mind to view the will of God in the orders of your superiors.
3. Be particularly faithful to your rule.
4. Recite the Psalm "Miserere" (Psalm 51 in the New American translation) on your knees.
5. Pray both the Our Father and Hail Mary once and "St. Joseph, pray for us" three times.

Aspiration

"St. Joseph, admirable model of obedience for those in authority, pray for us."

Scripture Verse

"Obey your leaders and defer to them, for they keep watch over you and will have to give an account, that they may fulfill their task with joy and not with sorrow . . ." (Hebrews 13:17)

Daily Meditation

"Let us contemplate St. Joseph as superior in his domestic capacity over Jesus and Marv, and admire his sweetness and humility. This is our model. Do we resemble him?"

Twenty-Fourth Day
St. Joseph, Cooperator in the Secret Designs of God

FIRST Point: The first great design in which St. Joseph cooperated was the sanctification of his soul. God created us without our cooperation, but He will not justify us without it. The greater the graces and privileges received, the more humble and earnest must be our endeavors to correspond with them. The creature is due no praise in himself for the concurring in these graces; on the contrary, he should fear lest sufficient cooperation has not been done on his part. St. Joseph understood perfectly well the necessity of this cooperation. Steeped with gratitude for the favors he had received, he strove only to correspond faithfully with them. We must likewise concur in the great design of our sanctification.

God has made known to us, by innumerable lights and graces, that He wishes us to become partakers of His happiness and glory. He purifies us from our faults, offers us every means of obtaining pardon, assists us in acquiring virtue—above all, the virtue of love. It was love that caused Him to reveal Himself to us, to assume our weak nature, becoming man for our salvation. "God is love" (1 John 4:8b). Do we comprehend the sublimity of our destiny and strive to attain it? The grace of God is necessary to advance in perfection, but our cooperation is required. "But by the grace of God I am what I am, and his grace to me has not been ineffective" (1 Corinthians 15:10).

Second Point: St. Joseph was made a participator in another great design of God: the care of Jesus, the Incarnate Word, and Mary, the most perfect of all creatures, masterpiece of the hand of God, purer and more exalted than the angels. The intimate, minute, and deep knowledge that he obtained of them was revealed to him by degrees. The angels, shepherds, and wise men, the voice of the multitude, the interior lights, but, above all, his thirty years' residence with them—which the angels themselves might have envied—served to show to St. Joseph the mysteries of grace and love attached to the persons of Jesus and Mary. This successive and gradual knowledge gave place to transports of admiration and delight. What must have been the happiness of St. Joseph in being so closely united to Him whom the angels and saints revere, and before whom they bow in lowly adoration! We may not be able to obtain the same degree of knowledge of these two beings, yet we can and should study daily to make progress in it. For have we not the Gospel explained and interpreted by the Church, and the lives of the saints that are reflections of the lives of Jesus and His holy mother? We have, above all, the Holy Eucharist; and where can be found more touching or more admirable remembrances of Nazareth?

Third Point: The third mystery in which St. Joseph was made a cooperator was that of which St. Paul speaks when he says, "Undeniably great is the mystery of devotion, Who was manifested in the flesh, vindicated in the spirit, seen by angels, proclaimed to the Gentiles, believed in throughout the world, taken up in glory" (1 Timothy 3:16). The Incarnation (united with the Redemption) for the salvation of the whole world, is the mystery in which St. Joseph, after the Blessed Virgin, became cooperator. He aided—by his obedience, zeal, and prudence—in the accomplishment of these designs; he contracted commitments with God that served to attach him to all mankind, rendering him in some manner responsible for each one of us—and even for the existence of our adorable Savior.

We, in turn, are obliged to cooperate by word and example in the fruits and effects of these mysteries. The mystery of the Incarnation is forcibly brought to the mind each day as we repeat the Angelus, "And the Word was made flesh, and dwelt among us." This part of the Angelus, fervently said, may be offered up by the pious soul in reparation for the affronts offered to the Redeemer by the taunts of the impious, the contempt of the unbeliever, the forgetfulness of the tepid, and the indifference of so many relaxed Christians.

Prayer

HOLY St. Joseph! My mind is deeply penetrated with the thoughts of these great truths; but I need the inspirations of divine grace to be faithful to the inspirations I have received. Obtain for me that, like you, I may faithfully cooperate in the designs of God. Amen.

Resolutions

1. Recall to mind the preceding reflections.
2. Carefully banish all distractions during prayer.
3. Avoid deliberate sins.
4. Recite both the Our Father and Hail Mary once and "St. Joseph, pray for us" three times.

Aspiration

"St. Joseph, faithful to divine grace, pray for us."

Scripture Verse

"But by the grace of God I am what I am, and his grace to me has not been ineffective." (1 Corinthians 15:10)

Daily Meditation

"The mystery of the Incarnation is forcibly brought to the mind each day as we repeat the Angelus, 'And the Word was made flesh, and dwelt among us.' This part of the

Angelus, fervently said, may be offered up by the pious soul in reparation for the affronts offered to the Redeemer by the taunts of the impious, the contempt of the unbeliever, the forgetfulness of the tepid, and the indifference of so many relaxed Christians."

Twenty-Fifth Day
St. Joseph, Model of Prudence

FIRST **Point:** Prudence is a virtue that causes us to use the most appropriate means in which to arrive at a proposed end. Prudence is a virtue old as the world. The Bible affords us admirable models of prudence. The first Joseph offers an example of this virtue unequalled in history, unless it be by the second Joseph, who stands out no less than the first by the prudent management of all confided to him. We have seen St. Joseph correspond with the designs of God in an admirable and perfect manner, and this correspondence was the fruit of his prudence. This is a necessary virtue, since one who is just and faithful to God is directed by it in the solution of the most delicate, important, and elevated questions. Our Savior Himself tells us to be prudent "as serpents and simple as doves" (Matthew 10:16). As the eyes of the servant never close completely, so prudence must always watch and rule our desires, words, and actions.

Second Point: There are two kinds of prudence—worldly prudence and a prudence coming from God; and it is necessary to discriminate between them. Worldly prudence, not having an object in view similar to Christian prudence, looks to the attainment of worldly advantages. It believes that the joy and happiness of man comes from their possession and cares not by what means this end be obtained, fearing only the law and the scorn of public opinion. The success that accompanies this worldly prudence seems to justify its practice; and its possessors fear nothing more than want of capacity, which they term a fault compromising them in the eyes of men; hence they avoid it. Can we rightfully accuse ourselves of practicing this prudence by following worldly motives to direct our actions? The first Joseph was chosen by Pharaoh to teach prudence to the wise men of the court. Let us learn this virtue from our father, St. Joseph.

Third Point: Christian prudence, unlike worldly prudence, proposes for its aim the eternal salvation of the soul, the glory of God, and the accomplishment of His adorable will. Even when regarding temporal, material, social, or political matters, Christian prudence always looks beyond the terrestrial aim. This is the first law of Christian prudence. As to the means made use of for the attainment of the proposed end, it draws them from the rules laid down in the Gospel, and from the examples contained therein. In selecting from them, it accepts only those which conscience regards as perfectly legitimate. Blending humility with these, it fears not any threatened misfortunes nor seeks to avoid them by making use of expedients injurious not only to sanctity but also to the dignity of a Christian. In working for God, a zeal enlightened by divine inspiration and directed by obedience is sure of success. St. Joseph is an admirable model of Christian prudence, the only one deserving of the name of "a prudent man" in its complete acceptance. St. Joseph was a simple, upright, and God-fearing man. His simplicity was not the result of a weak mind or judgment, but proceeded from the Dispenser of all graces, and was bestowed for our example. How do we imitate this sublime model?

Prayer

PRUDENT St. Joseph! Obtain for me the spirit of true simplicity. I have compromised by repeated infidelities—and have not made the proper use of—the means placed at my disposal for the attainment of this end by an all-wise Providence. Aid me, kind protector, to amend my life. Impress deeply on my heart the nothingness of earth and the importance of my eternal salvation. Amen.

Resolutions
1. During the course of the day, recall to mind the preceding reflections.
2. Follow the advice of a spiritual director or wise mentor-friend.
3. Recite both the Our Father and Hail Mary once and "St. Joseph, pray for us" three times.

Aspiration
"St. Joseph, perfect model of prudence, pray for us."

Scripture Verse
"Everyone who listens to these words of mine and acts on them will be like a wise [prudent] man who built his house on rock. . . . And everyone who listens to these words of mine but does not act on them will be like a fool who built his house on sand" (Matthew 7:24 & 26).

Daily Meditation
"St. Joseph is an admirable model of Christian prudence, the only one deserving of the name of "a prudent man" in its complete acceptance. St. Joseph was a simple, upright, and God-fearing man. His simplicity was not the result of a weak mind or judgment, but proceeded from the Dispenser of all graces, and was bestowed for our example. How do we imitate this sublime model?"

Twenty-Sixth Day
St. Joseph, Model of Chastity

FIRST **Point:** *The vow of virginity uniting Joseph and Mary* — We have already spoken of the title "Spouse of Mary" conferred on St. Joseph, a title that was the first and essential basis of his greatness. A virgin should have a virginal spouse; and there is every reason to believe, independently of Scripture, that St. Joseph had taken the vow of chastity. The bond was reciprocal, and the marriage of Joseph and Mary served only to unite them more closely and establish a mutual desire for the spiritual good of each other. "They are virgins uniting themselves," says the seventeenth-century French bishop Jacques-Benigne Bossuet, "and, like two bright stars, imparting their light to each other." St. Joseph united to the Blessed Virgin is a model that all married persons should strive to imitate. Regulating their lives, words, and actions in accordance with this model, they need not fear being led astray from the path of holiness.

Second Point: *Honor of the title of virgin* —Barrenness in a family was regarded by the Jews as a dishonor, or at least a severe trial. We read in the Old Testament of several just persons who accepted this trial with submission, but not without bitter regret. We have a touching example of this in the person of Anna, the mother of Samuel. Among the just who lived before the coming of our Savior, Scripture does not mention anyone who bound himself by vow to the practice of chastity. St. Joseph and the Blessed Virgin were the first. Let us congratulate and honor them as the recipients of this most glorious of all privileges.

Virginity is the highest state of life to which a creature can be called. If we have the happiness of being called to this state, let us thank our divine Savior for bestowing on us this greatest of graces. The married state is also holy and is ranked by Jesus Christ among the sacraments and sanctified in the Church by prayer. Virginity is holier, as is proved by the words of St. Paul: "So then, the one who marries his virgin does well; the one who does not marry her will do better" (1 Corinthians 7:38). Each individual is in duty bound to correspond as well as he is able to his vocation.

Third Point: *Reward of the virginity of St. Joseph* — The special privilege of being called the foster-father of Jesus Christ and the guardian of the Holy Virgin was a reward of St. Joseph's virginity, as was also the inexpressible honor given him of having Jesus repose on his virginal heart. By this first example of virginity given to the world, St. Joseph became the father and guardian of all who make a similar vow. Virgins, as spouses of Jesus, should carefully guard and cherish this virtue, inasmuch as they are obliged to instill a love and respect for it into the hearts of those under their care, and knowing that the more they themselves love, revere, and practice it, the greater will be their influence over others, and the greater their reward in eternity.

Prayer

O YOU who gave St. Joseph to Mary for a protector, and who favored the heart of this great saint by making it the first adorer of the Heart of Jesus in the bosom of His mother, grant that by his prayers and by imitating him, I may dwell with him in the heart of the Immaculate Virgin, there to adore God forever. Amen.

Resolutions

1. Recall to mind the preceding reflections.
2. Pray for humility.
3. Repeat occasionally the words of St. Paul: "Lord! What wilt thou have me to do?" (Acts 9:6, Douay-Rheims translation).
4. Observe modesty of the eyes.
5. Recite both the Our Father and Hail Mary once and "St. Joseph, pray for us" three times.

Aspiration

"St. Joseph, model of chaste souls, pray for us."

Scripture Verse

"Let marriage be honored among all and the marriage bed be kept undefiled, for God will judge the immoral and adulterers." (Hebrews 13:4)

Daily Meditation

"St. Joseph united to the Blessed Virgin is a model that all married persons should strive to imitate. Regulating their lives, words, and actions in accordance with this model, they need not fear being led astray from the path of holiness."

Twenty-Seventh Day
St. Joseph, Model of Purity

FIRST **Point:** *Beauty of the virtue of purity* — This heavenly virtue renders us dear to God and to men. "Blessed are the clean of heart, for they will see God" (Matthew 5:8). The perfume of this virtue is the most agreeable that can be offered to God. Purity assimilates man with the angels. In praising purity, it is St. Joseph we eulogize. "Virgin spouse of a virgin mother, pray for us. Preserve childhood free from violation in mind and heart, protect youth, support mature age; and may the aged, through your protection, add to their crowns gems of unsullied radiant purity. Amen."

Second Point: *The contrary vice* — Where is the painter who can find figures sufficiently dark and horrible with which to picture the contrary vice? God cursed it in the beginning of time in these terrible words: "My spirit shall not remain in man forever, since he is but flesh" (Genesis 6:3). God has punished it with fearful chastisements. In order to erase its stain from the earth, the Flood was sent; the cities of Sodom and Gomorrah were destroyed by fire; a whole tribe among the Israelites was annihilated on account of the sin of a few; David, the prophet king, chosen by God Himself, was rigorously chastised for his sin by the loss of his kingdom and the death of his son. Solomon, the wisest of kings, died leaving the world uncertain as to his destiny. The list of chastisements by which God punished, even here on earth, the vice of impurity is inexhaustible. If God sometimes delays the punishment, it is not the less certain nor terrible. Woe to him who, for the gratification of sensuality, brings sin and disgrace to an accomplice, or, worse still, to a poor victim. The punishment given on earth to such is remorse of conscience; and when this remorse is crushed, the neglect of religious practices follows, which is succeeded by loss of faith and, finally, that spiritual blindness that gives the sign of God's condemnation. "Chaste spouse of a virgin mother, pray for and protect us. Amen."

Third Point: *Means of preserving purity: watching, mortification, and prayer* — Our enemy goes about like a roaring lion, seeking whom he may devour; and he must be resisted with the arms of faith, which are fasting, watching, and prayer. Our Lord Himself tells us, when speaking of the demon of impurity, "This kind [of demon] can only come out through prayer [and through fasting]" (Mark 9:29). According to the interpretation of these words by the Church, fasting embraces all kinds of mortification and sacrifices. We have endeavored, during this month, to initiate you into the practice of mortification and sacrifices that could not injure your health nor interfere with the duties of your state of life. Let us strive to impress our minds with these thoughts and the valuable effects of these practices, so that we may derive lasting benefit from them, and make use of them in time of temptation, and at the same time be impressed with the truth that humility is necessary for us. The humble alone pass unsullied through this sort of temptation. Add to sacrifice, humility, and mortification morning and evening prayers, the Sign of the Cross in time of temptation, the invocation of the sweet names, "Jesus, Mary, and Joseph," and the words of the Lord's Prayer, "Lead us not into temptation." But all these will not suffice if we do not guard our imagination and senses. "Watch and pray that you may not undergo the test" (Mark 14:38). Parents, watch over your children; be their visible guardian angels, their second providences. Masters and mistresses, watch over and correct the disorders of your household; for nothing can escape the all-seeing eye of God, and you must account to Him at the tribunal of justice.

Prayer

O Guardian of Virgins and our holy father, St. Joseph, into whose faithful keeping were entrusted Christ Jesus, Innocence itself, and Mary, Virgin of virgins, I pray and beseech you by these dear pledges, Jesus and Mary, that, being preserved from all impurity, I may with spotless mind, pure heart and chaste body, serve Jesus and Mary most chastely all the days of my life. Grant me, dear Joseph, to run life's pathway in innocent fashion. Keep me safe under your blest patronage. Amen.

Resolutions

1. During the course of the day, recall to mind the preceding reflections.
2. Say three Hail Marys daily to preserve the virtue of purity.
3. Pray both the Our Father and Hail Mary once and "St. Joseph, pray for us" three times.

Aspiration

"St. Joseph, model of purity, pray for us."

Scripture Verse

"Be sober and vigilant. Your opponent the devil is prowling around like a roaring lion looking for [someone] to devour. Resist him, steadfast in faith, knowing that your fellow believers throughout the world undergo the same sufferings." (1 Peter 5:8-9)

Daily Meditation

"Add to sacrifice, humility, and mortification morning and evening prayers, the Sign of the Cross in time of temptation, the invocation of the sweet names, 'Jesus, Mary, and Joseph,' and the words of the Lord's Prayer, 'Lead us not into temptation.' But all these will not suffice if we do not guard our imagination and senses. 'Watch and pray that you may not undergo the test' (Mark 14:38)."

Twenty-Eighth Day
St. Joseph, Our Protector

F **IRST Point:** Since the first ages of the Church, the greatest and most illustrious saints and doctors have spoken in highest terms of St. Joseph. Sts. Gregory Nazianzen, John Chrysostom, John Damascene, Ambrose, and Augustine were his special promoters. In the course of centuries, the most eminent men have published his praises. Let it be sufficient for us to name Sts. Bernard, Thomas Aquinas, and Bernardine of Sienna. But the honor paid him by the Church has been fully developed since the heresies of Luther and Calvin. St. Teresa seems to have received a special mission from Providence for the promotion of devotion to St. Joseph. Here are her own words relative to this devotion: "I cannot, without wonder, admiration, and love, think of the great graces God has given me through the intercession of St. Joseph, and of the great perils of body and soul from which he has rescued me. It seems that God accords to other saints the power to assist us in certain circumstances, but I know from experience that St. Joseph can help us at all times and on all occasions; as though Jesus Christ wished to demonstrate that, as He was subject to him here on earth, He can now in heaven refuse him nothing. Other persons whom I advised to recommend themselves to his intercession have experienced his power in a similar manner, in consequence of which many now have great devotion to him, and daily feel more and more the truth of what I have asserted."

Second Point: St. Teresa's example has found imitators in every Catholic country, and we find devotion to St. Joseph rapidly increasing. Churches and chapels erected in his honor, religious associations organized under his patronage, congregations placed under his protection, the month of March especially consecrated to his remembrance, the widespread custom of invoking his name after the names of Jesus and Mary—all bear testimony of a special confidence in the protection of St. Joseph on the part of the children of the Catholic Church. The Church herself, through those who teach in her name, encourages and supports this generous impulse of confidence and affection. Taking only the pontificate of Pius IX, which is one of the most illustrious and glorious in the long series of popes, we see that almost immediately on his accession to the Chair of St. Peter, he established the feast of the "Patronage of St. Joseph." In his memorable address delivered in 1862, he recommended the Church and her wants to the powerful protection of St. Joseph; and later, by his authority, the entire Church was placed under his patronage.

Third Point: The charity of many has become cold; even faith itself is in danger of being lost in many souls; and new means from the treasury of divine Providence are needed to animate zeal, faith, and piety. The wants of the Church have become more pressing since the attacks of modern heresies and the so-called philosophy of rationalism. God gives clear proofs of the power of St. Joseph and His desire of having him honored and invoked by His children.

When friends fail on earth, win for yourselves friends in heaven. What patronage is more appropriate than his in our times? At present, all persons seem to desire rank and fortune. Let them picture to their minds the majestic figure of St. Joseph living contented in faith, hope, and charity. The working-classes are pressed down by disguised preachers of pantheism, atheism and socialism; and secret societies seek to increase their numbers, threatening the world with an overthrow unprecedented in history. Let us invoke this patron of workmen, himself an artisan, whose secret was that of an interior, hidden, humble life entirely devoted to the service of God and the love of his neighbor in union and company with Jesus and Mary.

Prayer

R EMEMBER, O amiable and powerful protector, St. Joseph, that, according to the testimony of your devoted servant, St. Teresa, no one ever implored your intercession with devotion and confidence without obtaining relief. Animated by this sweet and consoling hope, I come to you, O worthy spouse of the Virgin of virgins, and at your feet I seek your refuge and protection. O you who have borne the glorious title of Father of Jesus, reject not my humble prayer, but hear it favorably, and present it for me to Him who disdained not to be called your son, and who will not refuse your petition. Amen.

Resolutions

1. During the course of the day, recall to mind the preceding reflections.
2. Examine each action, and strive to acquire purity of intention in all you do.
3. Mortify your desire for drink, in union with the thirst endured by Jesus in His Passion.
4. Pray both the Our Father and Hail Mary once and "St. Joseph, pray for us" three times.

Aspiration

"St. Joseph, our special protector, pray for us."

Scripture Verse

"The fervent prayer of a righteous person is very powerful." (James 5:16b)

Daily Meditation

"It seems that God accords to other saints the power to assist us in certain circumstances, but I know from experience that St. Joseph can help us at all times and on all occasions; as though Jesus Christ wished to demonstrate that, as He was subject to him here on earth, He can now in heaven refuse him nothing." (St. Teresa of Avila)

Twenty-Ninth Day
St. Joseph, Patron of a Happy Death

PATRON of a Happy Death: Three reasons are given for conferring this title on St. Joseph.

First Point: He died in the arms of Jesus and Mary. To St. Joseph alone among men was given the consoling privilege of dying in the arms of Jesus and Mary. Sweet and tranquil must have been that death, attended as it was by those whose presence can calm the agitated soul, render less painful the final separation of the soul from the body, and alleviate the terrors of the awaiting judgment. Foolish indeed is the man who does not beg for this crowning grace of a happy death. According to a tradition confirmed by revelation, the death of St. Joseph occurred a short time previous to the commencement of the public ministry of our Savior. Nothing was yet known of the future wonders to be produced by Jesus—wonders that were to reflect so much glory on the poor family of Nazareth. Joseph died obscure and unknown—a perfect type of the Christian death in all its beauty, simplicity, and grandeur. Jesus died on the Cross, in torments and sufferings—a victim of expiation for the sins of men; and Mary, His mother, died fifteen years later, consumed with love and the ardent desire of beholding once more her divine Son, with whom she was so intimately united in soul.

The death of St. Joseph differed from these two holy deaths, in that his was accompanied with regret for leaving on earth those who formed his happiness, and who were one day to become the brightest ornaments of heaven. But he died filled with hope in the assurance of a blessed eternity, encouraged by the all-powerful love of Jesus and the sweet words of his Immaculate Spouse.

Let my soul die the death of the just. If in my last moments I feel a regret when leaving those I hold dear on earth, and the sorrow of that separation grieves my poor soul, dear patron, console me in the thought of the glorious reunion of all those united by the ties of blood, friendship, or faith, and whose happiness will be completed in heaven.

Second Point: St. Joseph is a powerful mediator with the heart of Jesus. After Jesus and Mary, what more powerful protector than St. Joseph can we invoke in the solemn and decisive moment on which all depends, when the soul in anguish calls on those who have the power of aiding and protecting her? Catholic reformer John Charlier of Gerson says that the prayers addressed by St. Joseph to Jesus and Mary have the force of a command, rather than the form of a supplication. The confidence of a Christian becomes animated and enlivened by these thoughts, and the name of St. Joseph becomes a sure and impenetrable shield against the shafts of hell, and an all-powerful safeguard in the terrors of death.

Third Point: St. Joseph was taught by Jesus and Mary to adopt us as his children. No mortal ever obtained so deep a knowledge of the hearts of Jesus and Mary as our dear father, St. Joseph. St. John was called the Beloved, the Apostle of preference, on account of his having reposed on the bosom of our Savior; but St. Joseph dwelt with Jesus for nearly thirty years in an intimacy that the angels might have envied and in the capacity of father. We should often reflect on what we owe St. Joseph in consideration of the numerous graces that he obtained from Jesus for all men, but especially for poor sinners. Moreover, in becoming the adopted father of Jesus, he became ours also; for are we not named, though infinitely unworthy, the brothers of

Jesus? Alas! Far more appropriate would be the title executioners of the world's Savior; for we daily become such by the commission of sin. Still, St. Joseph claims us for his children, and the tears and blood of his innocent Son render us dearer in his eyes, while the remembrance of Calvary serves to increase his loving and paternal tenderness towards us. If the affection of a father for his child shows itself most intensely at the hour of the death of the child, and if, as a Christian, he uses every means in his power to obtain for it the graces that accompany a happy death, what do you think must be the loving, earnest, anxious tenderness of our dear father, St. Joseph, when he sees one of his children on the point of being summoned before the just Judge? With fervor and love, he then offers on behalf of the dying the petitions addressed to himself.

Prayer

O LOVING father! Permit me to address you today as if it were the last day of my life. Inspire me with the sentiments I will experience on my deathbed; for then my soul will not seek for studied words, but will call on you from the depths of my own weakness and misery, pronouncing your name with love and confidence, and repeating often this little prayer: O dearest Father, whom I have loved so ardently, and so often invoked during life, pray for me now, and obtain for me the grace of a happy death. Amen.

Resolutions

1. During the course of the day, recall to mind the preceding reflections.
2. Desire death as the only means of complete union with God.
3. Recite on your knees the prayers for the faithful departed.

4. Recite both the Our Father and Hail Mary once and "St. Joseph, pray for us" three times.

Aspiration

"St. Joseph, our protector at the hour of death, pray for us."

Scripture Verse

". . . In love he [the Father] destined us for adoption to himself through Jesus Christ, in accord with the favor of his will." (Ephesians 1:4b-5)

Daily Meditation

"St. Joseph claims us for his children, and the tears and blood of his innocent Son render us dearer in his eyes, while the remembrance of Calvary serves to increase his loving and paternal tenderness towards us. If the affection of a father for his child shows itself most intensely at the hour of the death of the child, and if, as a Christian, he uses every means in his power to obtain for it the graces that accompany a happy death, what do you think must be the loving, earnest, anxious tenderness of our dear father, St. Joseph, when he sees one of his children on the point of being summoned before the just Judge?"

Thirtieth Day
Essential Preparations for a Happy Death

LET US again meditate on the important subject that yesterday engaged our attention, and, under the protection of St. Joseph, see what are the means of preparing ourselves for a happy death.

First Point: In order to die well, we must confess our sins and receive Holy Communion worthily. We may say that the best preparation for a happy death is a holy life; also, that a tender devotion to St. Joseph is a great security in one's last moments; and, finally, that all the practices and virtues to which the attention of the faithful has been called during this month, besides aiding them to live in a holy manner, will assist them to die happily. But there is still another means, of which we have not yet spoken, having reserved it for these last days, when the mind would naturally be better prepared to receive it as a truth. These means are Confession and Communion. The most ordinary, and yet the most essential, preparation for a happy death is the worthy reception of the last sacraments. If in our last illness we cannot receive these sacraments, we must endeavor to make up for this loss by our fervent desires and frequent aspirations. We ought daily to pray for the worthy reception of the last sacraments (Holy Viaticum).

Second Point: We should frequently approach the Sacraments of Penance and Holy Eucharist. Our Holy Mother, the Church, has set apart a specified time, during which we are to confess and communicate under pain of mortal sin. "Confess your sins at least once a year," she says, and adds, "Receive your Creator at Easter." Observe that she says, "at least once a year," expressing the desire she has of seeing her children approach more often.

The early Christians received Holy Communion every day, or at least as often as they assisted at the Holy Sacrifice. It is indeed a sad sight to see a parish whose members seldom or never approach the divine table through a scrupulous fear that they may offend our Lord. Equally sad is the knowledge that many forego the Sacrament of Penance and Reconciliation and receive the Body and Blood of Jesus Christ unworthily. It must not be fear—either of our loving Savior or of the loss of human respect—that guides our conscience on our worthy reception of the Blessed Sacrament. Rather, a heart full of love and devoid of false pride—a heart convinced of its own misery and nothingness—must seek for grace and virtue at the fount of mercy and love. As St. Francis de Sales stated, "We must fear God out of love, not love Him out of fear."

The more frequently and fervently we receive these two sacraments during life, the better prepared we will be to receive them at the hour of death. Let us, then, accustom ourselves to frequent Reconciliation and Holy Communion.

Third Point: We should endeavor to prepare ourselves to receive Holy Communion during life with the same dispositions we would wish to have at the hour of death. Let us adopt this practice in the Communion that is to crown the devotion of this beautiful month of St. Joseph. Let us approach the holy table with deep sentiments of humility, love, hope, and contrition that our Lord may not only condescend to abide in our hearts, but even desire to enter therein. We may be led to suppose that the thought of receiving our Lord for the last time would fill our hearts with fear and terror; but, on the contrary, it is the Holy Eucharist that makes the thought of death supportable and even sweet, enabling us to meet our Judge without fear, and stand in His august presence as a child before his father.

If much depends on the worthy reception of the sacraments, we ought to be exceedingly circumspect in our preparation, omitting nothing that could in the least degree contribute to make that preparation more devout and pleasing to God. The words used by a holy bishop immediately before his death are applicable to all when receiving our last sacraments (Holy Viaticum): "What need I fear in going to be judged by Him whom I love?"

Prayer

O GLORIOUS Joseph! My dear patron, inspire me with sentiments of the most ardent love towards Jesus in the Blessed Sacrament; and, as I am about to receive Him at the close of this your month, prepare, I beg you, my poor heart, that it may become an agreeable dwelling for Him. Grant that, by the worthy reception of this sacrament during life, I may merit the same grace at the hour of my death. Yes, dear St. Joseph, then more than ever will I need your assistance. Do not, I implore you, refuse it; stand near me in that fearful moment, and when the last struggle is over, accompany me to the judgment seat, and there, in union with the Blessed Virgin, plead for me until you have obtained a favorable sentence, that with you and my mother Mary I may enjoy God for all eternity. Amen.

Resolutions

1. During the course of the day, recall to mind the preceding reflections.
2. Detach yourself from the goods of the earth and mortify yourself today for that intention.

3. Bear with the faults of others.
4. Make some act of mortification in honor of the sufferings of Jesus.
5. Pray both the Our Father and Hail Mary once and "St. Joseph, pray for us" three times.

Invocation
"St. Joseph, patron of a happy death, pray for us."

Scripture Verse
"I heard a voice from heaven say, 'Write this: Blessed are the dead who die in the Lord from now on.' 'Yes,' said the Spirit, 'let them find rest from their labors, for their works accompany them.'" (Revelation 14:13)

Daily Meditation
"We may say that the best preparation for a happy death is a holy life."

Thirty-First Day
Benefits Derived from Devotion to St. Joseph

I N CLOSING this month of St. Joseph, we will form the resolution of reciting each day some prayer in his honor. We will endeavor to form the habit of frequently invoking the sweet names of Jesus, Mary, and Joseph, which will serve as aspirations, to be repeated during the day and in the hour of temptation, trial, and danger, when everything seems dark around us, and we feel abandoned by God and man. This practice, together with sacrifices offered daily through the merits of Jesus Christ, in union with His blessed mother and our dear father, St. Joseph, will aid us in keeping the resolutions formed during this month and serve as incentives to our spiritual progress. Various examples have been set before us for our encouragement, and from that we are to select those most suitable to our station in life as rules for our future conduct. The author of *The Imitation of Christ* justly observes, "Without sacrifice we cannot live the life of love."

Our progress in virtue will be according to the violence offered to self. Those souls, then, that are really desirous of advancing in perfection should endeavor to be penetrated with this precious lesson, applicable to every condition of life and suitable to the acquirement of all Christian virtue. When, at the close of day, we find that we have done nothing for the glory of God, we may justly say with the pagan emperor, Titus, who, regretting that no occasion of pleasing or benefiting others had been given him, exclaimed, "I have lost a day."

Following the example of many who are devoted to St. Joseph, let us choose Wednesday in each week as a day on which to render special homage to him and endeavor to attend the Holy Sacrifice of the Mass on that day. St. Francis de Sales calls the Mass the sun of spiritual exercises, center of Christian religion, heart of devotion, soul of piety, and abyss of divine charity, in which God, applying the merits of His Precious Blood, communicates to us His special graces and favors. If on that day we have not the happiness of making a sacramental Communion, we should at least make a spiritual one, which may be done by ardently desiring to receive our Lord at the moment when the priest and faithful communicate, offering to Him sentiments of humility, respect, and love, imploring the forgiveness of our sins and the grace of being more faithful in the future. In the end, during the course of the Way, beg St. Joseph to offer all your actions to the Blessed Virgin—and through her to Jesus—that they may be offered by this divine Mediator to His heavenly Father. We will strive to be faithful each year to the practices laid down in the month of St. Joseph, and during the month select a few days on which, in retreat, we may review the principal actions of our past life.

Prayer

ST. JOSEPH, most pure spouse of the Virgin Mary, pray for us daily to the Son of God, that armed with the weapons of His grace, we may fight as we ought in this life and be crowned by Him in death. Amen.

Invocation

"Jesus, Mary, and Joseph."

Scripture Verse

"So whether you eat or drink, or whatever you do, do everything for the glory of God." (1 Corinthians 10:31)

Daily Meditation

"When, at the close of day, we find that we have done nothing for the glory of God, we may justly say with the pagan emperor, Titus, who, regretting that no occasion of pleasing or benefiting others had been given him, exclaimed, 'I have lost a day.'"

Editor's Note: If you did not consecrate yourself to our good St. Joseph on his feast day this month and wish to do so, pray the Act of Consecration on page 133 for this purpose. This consecration should be renewed each year on his feast day (March 19). You may wish to renew this consecration on the first Wednesday of each month by praying the Act of Consecration to St. Joseph then. If desired, you may pray the Prayer to St. Joseph for Our Family each Wednesday as well.

Traditional Prayers Honoring
St. Joseph

Act of Consecration to St. Joseph
Litany of St. Joseph
Prayer to St. Joseph
Novena to St. Joseph
Thirty Days' Prayer to St. Joseph
Wednesday Prayer to St. Joseph
Nine First Wednesdays of St. Joseph
Prayer to St. Joseph for Our Family

Act of Consecration to St. Joseph

O GLORIOUS St. Joseph! I present myself before you to consecrate the remainder of my life to you. Accept, I beseech you, this poor offering, and, in union with your Immaculate Spouse, present it to Jesus, your divine Son, by Him to be offered to His heavenly Father, to receive the smile of approval and the grace of final perseverance. I consecrate to you my thoughts that they may be always subject to reason and guided by faith. Preserve me from being biased in my opinions by the vain judgments of a wicked, deceitful world. I consecrate to you my heart, with its emotions, desires, and affections; it needs more restraint than my understanding, on account of its many attractions, preferences, and weaknesses. I consecrate my senses to you, together with all the actions in which they participate. Grant that, in being organs of the soul, they may be used in obtaining the greater honor and glory of God. Instill into my soul a love of virtue that will be the governing principle of all my actions, and guard me by your grace and love against all the attacks of the evil one. I am surrounded by dangers that threaten to prove my ruin; even the little good I do is so full of self-love that it corrupts my best intentions. Overwhelmed with fear at the sight of so many obstacles, I cast myself before you, imploring your assistance, and renewing the offerings already made, as also the resolution of doing all for Jesus, in Him and through Him, that, serving Him faithfully in this life, I may enjoy Him for all eternity. Amen.

Litany of St. Joseph

L ORD, have mercy. *Lord, have mercy.*
Christ, have mercy. *Christ, have mercy.*
Lord, have mercy. *Lord, have mercy.*
Christ, hear us. *Christ, graciously hear us.*
God, the Father of Heaven, *have mercy on us.*
God the Son, Redeemer of the world, *have mercy on us.*
God the Holy Spirit, *have mercy on us.*
Holy Trinity, one God, *have mercy on us.*
Holy Mary, Spouse of Joseph, *pray for us.*
Holy Joseph, Spouse of the Virgin Mary, *pray for us.*
Foster-father of Jesus, *pray for us.*
Man according to God's own heart, *pray for us.*
Faithful and prudent servant, *pray for us.*
Guardian of the virginity of Mary, *pray for us.*
Companion and solace of Mary, *pray for us.*
Most pure in virginity, *pray for us.*
Most profound in humility, *pray for us.*
Most fervent in charity, *pray for us.*
Most exalted in contemplation, *pray for us.*
Who was declared to be a just man by the testimony of the
  Holy Spirit Himself, *pray for us.*
Who was enlightened above all in heavenly mysteries,
  pray for us.
Who was the chosen minister of the counsels of the Most
  High, *pray for us.*
Who was taught from above the mystery of the Incarnate
  Word, *pray for us.*
Who journeyed to Bethlehem with Mary, your spouse, *pray
  for us.*
Who, finding no place in the inn, established yourself in a
  stable, *pray for us.*

Who was thought worthy to be present when Christ was born and laid in a manger, *pray for us.*

Who bore in your arms the Son of God, *pray for us.*

Who received the Blood of Jesus at His circumcision, *pray for us.*

Who presented Him to His Father in the Temple, with Mary, His mother, *pray for us.*

Who, at the warning of the angel, journeyed immediately into Egypt with the Child and His mother, *pray for us.*

Who, when Herod was dead, returned with them into the land of Israel, *pray for us.*

Who for three days, with Mary, His mother, sought sorrowing the Child Jesus when He was lost at Jerusalem, *pray for us.*

Who, after three days, with joy found Him sitting in the midst of the doctors, *pray for us.*

Who had the Lord of lords subject to you on the earth, *pray for us.*

Who was the happy witness of His hidden life and sacred words, *pray for us.*

Who died in the arms of Jesus and Mary, *pray for us.*

Whose praise is in the Gospel: The spouse of Mary, of whom was born Jesus, *pray for us.*

Humble imitator of the Incarnate Word, *pray for us.*

Powerful support of the Church, *pray for us.*

Our advocate, St. Joseph, *hear us.*

Our patron, St. Joseph, *graciously hear us.*

In all our necessities, *St. Joseph, help us.*

In all our distresses, *St. Joseph, help us.*

In the hour of death, *St. Joseph, help us.*

Through your most chaste espousals, *St. Joseph, help us.*

Through your paternal care and fidelity, *St. Joseph, help us.*

Through your love of Jesus and Mary, *St. Joseph, help us.*

Through your labors and toils, *St. Joseph, help us.*

Through all your virtues, *St. Joseph, help us.*

Through your exalted honor and eternal blessedness, *St. Joseph, help us.*

Through your faithful intercession, *we beseech you, hear us.*

That you would obtain for us from Jesus the pardon of our sin, *we beseech you, hear us.*

That you would commend us faithfully to Jesus and Mary, *we beseech you, hear us.*

That you would obtain for all, both virgins and married, the chastity belonging to their state, *we beseech you, hear us.*

That you would obtain for all congregations perfect love and unity, *we beseech you, hear us.*

That you would direct all rulers in the government of their subjects, *we beseech you, hear us.*

That you would assist all parents in the Christian education of their children, *we beseech you, hear us.*

That you would protect all those that rely upon your patronage, *we beseech you, hear us.*

That you would support, with your paternal help, all congregations instituted under your name and patronage, *we beseech you, hear us.*

That you would visit and stand by us with Jesus and Mary in the last moment of our life, *we beseech you, hear us.*

That you would assist, by your prayers and intercession, all the faithful departed, *we beseech you, hear us.*

O chaste spouse of Mary, *we beseech you, hear us.*

O faithful foster-father of Jesus, *we beseech you, hear us.*

Holy Joseph, *we beseech you, hear us.*

Lamb of God, who takes away the sins the world, *spare us, O Lord.*

Lamb of God, who takes away the sins of the world, *graciously hear us, O Lord.*

Lamb of God, who takes away the sins of the world, *have mercy on us.*

Christ, hear us. *Christ, graciously hear us.*

Pray for us, O blessed Joseph, *that we may be made worthy of the promises of Christ.*

Let us pray.

O GOD, who chose St. Joseph to be the spouse of Blessed Mary, ever virgin, and to be the guardian and foster-father of your beloved Son, our Lord Jesus Christ, we humbly beseech you to grant us, through his patronage and merits, such purity of mind and body that, being clean from every stain and clothed with the true marriage-garment, we may, by your great mercy, be admitted to the heavenly nuptials, through the same Jesus Christ, our Lord. Amen.

O God, who in your divine Providence chose blessed Joseph to be the spouse of your most holy mother, grant, we beseech you, that we may be made worthy to receive him for our intercessor in heaven whom on earth we venerate as our holy protector, who lives and reigns, world without end. Amen.

Prayer to St. Joseph to Obtain the Spirit of Our Vocation

G LORIOUS St. Joseph, chaste spouse of Mary, our good mother, and foster-father of Jesus, our amiable saint; humbly prostrate at your feet, we choose you anew for our good father, and beg you to receive us among the members of your privileged children.

We thank you with our whole heart for having given us a place in this holy family, of which you are the protector as the father. Burning with the desire of responding worthily to our holy vocation, we call upon you, with the most loving confidence, to obtain for us its spirit and virtues. Yes, great saint, grant that, following your example, we may every day make new progress in humility, obedience, recollection, the spirit of poverty, and, above all, in the love of Jesus and Mary.

May we, like you, find our delight in serving this sweet Jesus in the person of His suffering members, as you had the happiness of serving Him in His own person. We ask you to crown all your favors by obtaining for us the grace to die like you in the arms of Jesus and Mary that we may go to share your happiness in the company of our beloved brothers and sisters who have gone before us, and who await us near you in the heavenly country. Amen.

Novena to St. Joseph

Directions for Each Day of the Novena — If desired, begin each day with the Litany of the Saints. Then, say one of the following prayers, recite the Our Father and the Hail Mary three times, and conclude by the votive oblation prayer to St. Joseph found on page 144.

First Day

B LESSED St. Joseph, born to be the guardian of Jesus, the protector and consoler of Mary, make powerful intercession for me, that my pious resolutions may not prove fruitless, that I may be born to an interior and spiritual life, that I may have such an increase of sanctity, so ardent a love of purity, so great a conviction of my own vileness, so clear a light of the emptiness and vanity of worldly grandeur, as to esteem and relish only things that are eternal. Through our Lord Jesus Christ. Amen.

Second Day

O MNIPOTENT Creator, whose unerring Providence adds joy every moment to the angels in heaven and to the saints upon earth, I most humbly beg, through the intercession of St. Joseph, that I may cheerfully accept and rejoice in everything that comes from your fatherly hand; that I may be vigorous in executing your divine will, and glorify you in my present state. Grant me the true spirit of mortification to subdue my stubborn passions, to satisfy for what is past, and to be preserved from future dangers. Grant that, by purity of intention, the most humble of my actions may be acceptable to you, as was the mite of the poor woman that was put into the treasury of the Temple. Through Jesus Christ our Lord. Amen.

Third Day

OMNIPOTENT God, at whose command every tree produces fruit of its kind, grant, through the intercession of Mary and Joseph, that I may serve you faithfully in the state in which you have placed me. I firmly believe all you have revealed; protect me, lest I should be found among the number of those foolish virgins who carried lamps without oil. Assist me with your powerful grace, that I may be humble, charitable, and chaste, and not like the barren fig tree, fit only to become fuel for eternal flames. This grace I implore through the infinite merits of Jesus, my Savior. Amen.

Fourth Day

HOLY SPIRIT, God of all comfort, if you see it expedient for the security of my salvation that I should be oppressed with tribulation, permit me not to fall. Infinite power, bear me up; you know my weakness. Favor me with your grace that I may be compassionate towards my neighbor, and govern myself with the same spirit of mercy and charity as if the case were my own. I deplore my critical temper, and resolve to be upon my guard. I give you thanks for inspiring me with the resolution of becoming better; but of myself, I am not able to persevere in my good intentions. I beg your assistance that I may fulfill what you command; and then, dear Lord, command what you please. Afflict me with such crosses as I can endure that I may satisfy at least a part of the great debt due to your divine justice. Grant, through the intercession of St. Joseph, that after my temporal trials, whether exterior or interior, I may find that permanent joy with which you render him and his Immaculate Spouse eternally happy. Through the merits of our Lord Jesus Christ, who lives and reigns with you and the Holy Spirit, one God, forever and ever. Amen.

Fifth Day

O INFINITE God, how truly may it be said of me, "An ox knows its owner, and an ass, its master's manger; but Israel does not know, my people has not understood" (Isaiah 1:3). I admire your love and charity. I am ashamed of my tepidity and ingratitude. Infinite Goodness, I come too late to love you; but although it be the eleventh hour, bestow on me the promised reward; be to me a Savior. You who have bled for me, let me partake of your eternal charity. Grant that through the intercession of St. Joseph, my good resolutions may be perfected. I also beg that when I adore you in the Most Blessed Sacrament, I may be favored with the same sentiments of adoration, love, and thanksgiving that St. Joseph experienced when he received you from Simeon to restore you to your blessed mother. Amen.

Sixth Day

JESUS, my Maker and my Master, without whose merciful assistance I walk in darkness and perish, I most humbly beg, through the intercession of St. Joseph, that you will grant me the grace to escape from the servitude of sin, under which I have so long groaned, in order that I may enjoy the liberty of your faithful servants. I have frequently experienced your goodness, and I know your power; my trust is in both. Oh, grant me constancy to despise the allurements of the world and to remain undaunted under afflicting terrors. My dear Redeemer, I have too often lost you by sin; I have willingly and willfully parted with you to follow my corrupt inclinations. O God, who came to seek sinners, take pity on me, the greatest of sinners. You are now pleased to bless me with such a true sense of my former offenses that I grieve not so much for the fear of punishment as for the misfortune of having offended you, the center of all goodness.

I steadfastly purpose, through your grace, to seek you seriously by the reformation of my life, that I may find you in the heavenly Jerusalem reigning with the Father and the Holy Spirit, world without end. Amen.

Seventh Day

OMNIPOTENT God, who descended from heaven to bring fire on earth, inflame my frozen heart, that I may imitate the virtues of St. Joseph. As a poor wretch at the gate of some noble and generous prince expecting an alms, so I appear before you, wounded in all my senses by sin, and imploring charity in my great distress. I grieve for what is passed, not because I fear, but because I love. Nothing has succeeded with me, because I never consulted you as I ought. I hope, O Lord, that I do not come too late. I beg, through the intercession of St. Joseph, that I may avoid evil and do good; that I may leave the broad road of iniquity, and walk in the narrow road that leads to eternal happiness; that I may consecrate the remaining days of my short life to your honor, and attain the end for which I was created—to admire, praise, and love you forever and ever. Amen.

Eighth Day

O MOST glorious patriarch, my dear patron, blessed are the eyes that see what you now see. Through the infinite merits of Christ, and by your powerful intercession, I hope, with holy Job, that in my flesh I shall see God my Savior. Stretch out, in favor of your unworthy admirer, those happy arms that so often bore the Son of God and provided for Him. Petition that I may live, as I wish to die, always in the divine favor. I humbly implore you to implore your Immaculate Spouse to unite her supplications with yours that I may be of the blessed number of the elect. I most sincerely desire that you may be present at the dreadful hour of my death, and that the last words uttered by my parting breath may be "Jesus, Mary, and Joseph."

Your mercy is above all your works. O most holy Trinity! I now appeal from the tribunal of your justice, and prostrate myself before the throne of your mercy, to obtain the pardon of my sins, and grace to persevere in keeping your commandments to the end of my life. Who lives and reigns, one God forever and ever. Amen.

Ninth Day

HOLY St. Joseph, you who are that good and faithful servant to whom God committed the care of His family; whom he appointed guardian and protector of the life of Jesus Christ, the comfort and support of His holy mother, and the cooperator of His great design for the redemption of mankind; you who had the happiness of living with Jesus and Mary, and of dying in their arms; chaste spouse of the Mother of God, model and patron of pure souls, humble, patient, and reserved, be moved with the confidence we place in your intercession, and accept with kindness this testimony of our devotion.

We give thanks to God for the extraordinary favor He has been pleased to confer on you, and we ask Him, through your intercession, to enable us to imitate your virtues. Pray for us, then, O great saint, and by that love which you had for Jesus and Mary, and by the love which they had for you, obtain for us the incomparable happiness of living and dying in the love of Jesus and Mary. Amen.

A Votive Oblation to St. Joseph to Choose Him for Our Patron

HOLY Joseph, virgin spouse of the Virgin Mother of God, most glorious advocate of all who are in danger or in their last agony, and most faithful protector of all the servants of Mary, your dearest spouse, I, [state your name], in the presence of Jesus and Mary, do, from this moment, choose you for my powerful patron and advocate, in order that I may obtain the grace of a most happy death; I firmly resolve and purpose never to forsake you, nor to say or do anything against your honor. Receive me, therefore, as your constant servant, and recommend me to the constant protection of Mary, your dearest spouse, and to the everlasting mercies of Jesus, my Savior. Assist me in all the actions of my life; I now offer them to the greater and everlasting glory of Jesus and Mary, as well as to your own. Amen.

Thirty Days' Prayer to St. Joseph, Chaste Spouse of the Ever Immaculate and Blessed Virgin Mary, and Foster-Father of Jesus Christ to Obtain a Happy Death and Other Good Intentions

E VER blessed and glorious Joseph, kind and indulgent father, and compassionate friend of all in sorrow, through that bitter grief with which your heart was saturated when you beheld the sufferings of the Infant Savior, and in prophetic view contemplated His most ignominious Passion and Death, take pity, I beseech you, on my poverty and necessities: counsel me in my doubts, and console me in all my anxieties. You are the good father and protector of orphans, the advocate of the defenseless, the patron of those who are in need and desolation. Do not, then, disregard the petition of your poor child; my sins have drawn down upon me the just displeasure of my God, and hence I am surrounded with sorrows. To you, O amiable guardian of the poor neglected family of Nazareth, do I fly for shelter and protection. Listen, then, I beg you, with a father's solicitude, to the earnest prayer of your poor supplicant, and obtain for me the objects of my petition. I ask it by the infinite mercy of the eternal Son of God, which induced Him to assume our nature, and be born into this world of sorrow. I ask it by the grief which filled your heart when, ignorant of the mystery wrought in your Immaculate Spouse, you feared you should be separated from her.

I ask it by that weariness, solicitude, and suffering that you endured when you searched in vain at the inns of Bethlehem a shelter for the sacred Virgin and a birth place for the Infant God, and when, being everywhere refused, you were obliged to consent that the Queen of Heaven should give birth to the world's Redeemer in a wretched stable. I ask it by that most sad and painful duty imposed on you when, the divine Child being eight days old, you were obliged to inflict a deep wound on His tender body, and thus be the first to make flow that sacred Blood that was to wash away the sins of the world. I ask it by the sweetness and power of that sacred name, Jesus, which you conferred on the adorable Infant. I ask it by that mortal anguish inflicted on you by the prophecy of holy Simeon, which declared the Child Jesus and His holy Mother the future victims of their love and our sins. I ask it through that sorrow and anguish that filled your soul when the angel declared to you that the life of the Child Jesus was sought by His enemies, from whose unholy designs you were obliged to fly with Him and His blessed mother into Egypt. I ask it by all the pains, fatigues, and toils of that long and perilous pilgrimage. I ask it by all the sorrows you endured when in Egypt you were not able, even by the sweat of your brow, to obtain poor food and clothing for your most poor family. I ask it by all the grief you felt each time the divine Child asked for a morsel of bread, and you had it not to give Him. I ask it by all your solicitude to preserve the sacred Child and the Immaculate Mary during your second journey, when you were ordered to return to your native country. I ask it by your peaceful dwelling in Nazareth, in which so many joys and sorrows were mingled. I ask it by your extreme affliction in being three days deprived of the company of the adorable Child. I ask it by your joy at finding Him in the Temple, and by the indescribable consolation imparted to you in the cottage of Nazareth with the company and society of the little Jesus. I ask it by that wonderful condescension by which He subjected Himself to your will. I ask it through that sorrowful view, continually in your mind, of all your Jesus was to suffer. I ask it by that painful contemplation that made you foresee the divine little hands and feet, now so active in serving you, one day to be pierced with cruel nails; that head, which rested gently on your bosom, crowned with sharp thorns; that delicate body, which you tenderly folded in your mantle and pressed to your heart, stripped and extended on a cross. I ask it by that heroic sacrifice of your will and best affections, by which you offered up to the eternal Father the last awful moment when the Man-God was to expire for our salvation. I ask it by that perfect love and conformity with which you received the divine order to depart from this life and from the company of Jesus and Mary. I ask it by that exceedingly great joy that filled your soul when the Redeemer of the world, triumphant over death and hell, entered into the possession of His kingdom, and conducted you also into it with special honors. I ask it through Mary's glorious Assumption, and through that everlasting bliss which with her you will eternally derive from the presence of God.

O good father, I beseech you, by all your sufferings, sorrows, and joys, to hear me, and to obtain the grant of my earnest petitions. [Here name them or reflect on them.] Obtain for all those who have asked your prayers all that is useful to them in the designs of God. And finally, my dear protector, I ask that you be with me and all who are dear to me in our last moments, that we may eternally chant the praises of Jesus, Mary, and Joseph. Amen.

Editor's Note: This prayer may be prayed for a special intention any thirty days of the year in honor of the thirty years St. Joseph spent with Jesus and Mary.

Wednesday Prayer to St. Joseph

Editor's Note: Just as the month of March is dedicated to St. Joseph, so too is Wednesday of each week. The following ancient prayer—purportedly dating back to the fiftieth year of our Lord and Savior—can be prayed each Wednesday in honor of St. Joseph.

O St. Joseph, whose protection is so great, so strong, so prompt before the throne of God, I place in you all my interests and desires. O St. Joseph, assist me by your powerful intercession and obtain for me all spiritual blessings through your foster Son, Jesus Christ our Lord, so that, having engaged here below your heavenly power, I may offer you my thanksgiving and homage. O St. Joseph, I never weary contemplating you and Jesus asleep in your arms. I dare not approach while He reposes near your heart. Press Him in my name and kiss His fine head for me, and ask Him to return the kiss when I draw my dying breath. St. Joseph, patron of departing souls, pray for me. Amen.

Nine First Wednesdays of St. Joseph

You may make the devotion of the Nine First Wednesdays to St. Joseph in a manner similar to the Nine First Fridays to the Sacred Heart of Jesus by offering your first Wednesday Mass and Communion to St. Joseph for the intention of honoring St. Joseph and requesting a happy death for yourself, your loved ones, and those dying souls who have no one to pray for them.

Prayer to St. Joseph for Our Family

G lorious St. Joseph! You, to whom God confided the care of the two personas He most loved on earth, forget not that we too have been entrusted to your care.

You who are our protector and our father, take, we pray, our interests into your own hands, but above all, watch over all the concerns of our souls.

O virtuous guardian of the Holy Family, by your powerful intercession, *make us a family of saints.* And since to merit your favors, we must strive to imitate your virtues, obtain for us all a sincere will to walk in your footsteps and to be like you, full of love for Jesus and Mary and faithful to all our other duties.

You are too jealous of the glory of God and our salvation to refuse to receive our prayers.

O beloved head of the Holy Family, graciously hear us. Amen.

More RACE for Heaven Products

RACE for Heaven study guides use the saint biographies of Mary Fabyan Windeatt to teach the Catholic faith to all members of your family. Written with your family's various learning levels in mind, these flexible study guides succeed as stand-alone unit studies or supplements to your regular curriculum. Thirty to sixty minutes per day will allow your family to experience:

☑ The spirituality and holy habits of the saints
☑ Lively family discussions on important faith topics
☑ Increased critical thinking and reading comprehension skills
☑ Quality read-aloud time with Catholic "living books"
☑ Enhanced knowledge of Catholic doctrine and the Bible
☑ History and geography incorporated into saintly literature
☑ Writing projects based on secular and Catholic historical events and characters

Purchase these guides individually or in the following grade-level packages. (Grades are determined solely on the length of each book in the series.)

Grades 3-4: *St. Thomas Aquinas, The Story of the "Dumb Ox"; St. Catherine of Siena, The Girl Who Saw Saints in the Sky; Patron Saint of First Communicants, The Story of Blessed Imelda Lambertini;* and *The Miraculous Medal, The Story of Our Lady's Appearances to St. Catherine Labouré*

Grade 5: *St. Rose, First Canonized Saint of the Americas; St. Martin de Porres, The Story of the Little Doctor of Lima, Peru; King David and His Songs, A Story of the Psalms;* and *Blessed Marie of New France, The Story of the First Missionary Sisters in Canada*

151

Grade 6: *St. Dominic, Preacher of the Rosary and Founder of the Dominicans; St. Benedict, The Story of the Father of the Western Monks; The Children of Fatima and Our Lady's Message to the World;* and *St. John Masias, Marvelous Dominican Gate-keeper of Lima, Peru*

Grade 7: *The Little Flower, The Story of St. Therese of the Child Jesus; St. Hyacinth, The Story of the Apostle of the North; The Curé of Ars, The Story of St. John Vianney, Patron Saint of Parish Priests;* and *St. Louis de Montfort, The Story of Our Lady's Slave*

Grade 8: *Pauline Jaricot, Foundress of the Living Rosary and the Society for the Propagation of Faith; St. Francis Solano, Wonder-Worker of the New World and Apostle of Argentina and Peru; St. Paul the Apostle, The Story of the Apostle to the Gentiles;* and *St. Margaret Mary, Apostle of the Sacred Heart*

The Windeatt Dictionary: Pre-Vatican II Terms and Catholic Words from Mary Fabyan Windeatt's Saint Biographies explains over 450 Catholic terms and expressions used in this popular saint biography series. Indispensable in expanding knowledge and practice of the Catholic faith, this book provides a ready access for the Catholic vocabulary words used in the RACE for Heaven Windeatt study guides. This dictionary also includes a Catholic book report resource that contains suggestions for forty-five Catholic book reports: fourteen writing projects, ten book report activities, and twenty-one topics for saint biographies.

Graced Encounters with Mary Fabyan Windeatt's Saints: 344 Ways to Imitate the Holy Habits of the Saints is a compilation of the "Growing in Holiness" sections of RACE for Heaven's Catholic study guides for the Windeatt saint biography series and presents 344 examples of saintly behavior, one for nearly every chapter in each of these twenty biographies. Enhance your encounter with the saints by practicing the models of devotion, service, penance, prayer, and virtue offered in this guide.

Bedtime Bible Stories for Catholic Children: Loving Jesus through His Word contains twenty discussions of Bible stories that were originally published in serial form in a Catholic children's magazine. Their author stated, "The tales are extremely simple and unadorned. They are real conversations of a real child and her mother." Due to popular demand, the series was later (1910) published as a book, *Bible Stories Told to "Toddles."* The engaging conversational style of this book lends itself well as a bedtime read-aloud that allows Jesus to come alive in the Gospels. The study aids include discussion questions to help foster spiritual conversation, Bible excerpts relevant to the presented story, "Growing in Holiness" suggestions for living the Gospel message in our daily lives, and short catechism lessons for both children and adults.

Communion with the Saints: A Family Preparation Program for First Communion and Beyond in the Spirit of St. Therese imitates St. Therese of the Child Jesus and her family who studied and prayed for sixty-nine days in anticipation of Therese's First Holy Communion. Modeling this preparation, the *Communion with the Saints* program will help any family find renewed fervor in the reception of the Eucharist. This resource includes a chapter-by-chapter study of the following four books:

- *The Little Flower, The Story of Saint Therese of the Child Jesus*—to provide the foundation of God's love for us and to encourage a desire for holiness

- *The Children of Fatima and Our Lady's Message to the World*—to show the sinfulness of our world and the need to avoid sin

- *The Patron Saint of First Communicants, The Story of Blessed Imelda Lambertini*—to inspire devotion to the Sacrament of Holy Communion
- *The King of the Golden City* by Mother Mary Loyola —to illustrate Jesus' Presence as a source of grace necessary to live a holy life

Each of the sixty-nine days of preparation includes read-aloud selections with enrichment activities, meditational readings, catechism lessons, and plenty of practical application to promote a growth in holiness and sanctity. Weekend suggestions include a list of over thirty-five family projects. (The use of either *My First Communion Journal in Imitation of St. Therese or My First Communion Journal in Imitation of St. Paul* is encouraged with this program.)

My First Communion Journal in Imitation of Saint Therese the Little Flower replicates the copybook made for Therese Martin by her older sister to help Therese prepare for her First Holy Communion. Each day of her sixty-nine day preparation period Therese recorded the number of times she recited the included prayers and aspirations. By using her "sacrifice beads," she counted each time she overcame her own desires in order to please Jesus. Although this book is not an exact replica of the copybook used by Therese, it does contain many of the same prayers and aspirations she used, the same idea of flowers inspiring virtue, and the same method of recording prayers recited and sacrifices made. It is up to you to decorate and complete this journal, imitating Therese's heroic efforts by raising your mind and heart to Jesus and by humbling yourself with small sacrifices. Learn as well to mimic St. Therese's love and knowledge of Scripture as you meditate on—or even memorize—the biblical passages that are provided for reflection. Used on its own or in conjunction with the *Communion with the Saints* program, this journal will be a cherished First Communion keepsake.

My First Communion Journal in Imitation of St. Paul: Putting on the Armor of God is similar to the previous journal in that it uses the same method of encouraging—and recording—daily prayers and mortifications. However, instead of using flowers to illustrate virtues, this resource uses the battle model St. Paul describes in Ephesians 6:10-17. First communicants are encouraged to arm themselves with virtues and spiritual weapons in order to fight as soldiers of Christ. The scriptural words of Jesus and St. Paul are reflected on frequently to encourage the imitation of the actions and love of Jesus and to inspire a love and knowledge of Holy Scripture.

The King of the Golden City Study Edition is a new edition of a book that was originally published in 1921. This treasure of a book was written in response to a student's appeal for instructions along with "little stories" to help her prepare for Holy Communion. To fulfill this request, Mother Loyola of the Bar Convent in York, England, wrote a simple story that illustrates Jesus' desire to share an intimate relationship with each one of His children. This new edition contains some updated language but, quite deliberately, does not contain any pictures. Readers, as they progress through this story, will form a mental image of their King, one as unique and personal as their own relationship with Him. The study sections assist with the allegory, connect to the Bible as well as to the catechism, and explore the art of prayer in the spirit of the three Carmelite Doctors of the Church. Although written over eighty-five years ago for a young child, this book remains a timeless masterpiece of Catholic literature suitable for all ages. (Also available as a study guide only)

The Good Shepherd and His Little Lambs Study Edition is a simply told Catholic tale of four children who meet with their beloved aunt for "First Communion talks." More than a story, it is a First Communion primer that takes the tenets of the catechism and, through naturally-flowing conversations, relates them in the language of little ones to authentic Christian living. As Mrs. Bosch explains, "We might learn the catechism all the way through beautifully, and at the end find ourselves still very stiff and clumsy about loving our Lord. When He comes to us, we don't want to welcome Him into our souls only with answers out of the catechism, do we?" Enriched by appropriate Biblical passages, points of doctrine, and prayers, this story-primer is an enjoyable and effective read-aloud that will prepare the Good Shepherd's little lambs to worthily receive Him in the Holy Eucharist.

I Talk with God: The Art of Prayer and Meditation for Catholic Children strives to instill in young Catholics not only a love of our Lord in the Holy Eucharist but also a love of prayer and a practical knowledge of the art of meditation. This prayer book explores the many ways to pray: out loud (vocal prayer), in the silence of your heart, using pictures and images or Bible stories, or while exploring God outdoors in His wonderful creation. As you progress through this book—from discovering what prayer is to reading and reciting simple prayers to understanding meditation and then to helps for deeper meditation—you will see that prayer and meditation often go together and that meditation is nothing more than "prayerful reflection" or holy thinking. With this prayer book, each day young Catholics can love God more and learn to hear His loving voice and follow His holy will.

A Reconciliation Reader-Retreat: Read-Aloud Lessons, Stories, and Poems for Young Catholics Preparing for Confession provides a basic doctrinal explanation and review of the Sacrament of Reconciliation as well as a Gospel examination of conscience—a seven-day read-aloud formation retreat. To help the lessons come alive and to enable young Catholics to more readily apply these doctrines to their own daily lives, the lessons have been supplemented with pertinent short stories and poems. Each lesson contains reflection questions, a family prayer, and a "Gospel Examination of Conscience" that is formulated according to the dictates of the *Catechism of the Catholic Church*. This reader-retreat will not only enrich and deepen the sacramental experience for each member of your family but it will also provide several tools to help you recommit to leading a virtuous life and to grow together in holiness.

Devotion to St. Joseph: Read-Aloud Stories, Poems, and Prayers for Catholic Children encourages children—through stories by such renowned authors as Sr. Margaret Patrice, Wilfrid Sheed, Catherine Beebe, Sr. Mary Charitas, and Mary Mannix and poems by Rev. Edward F. Garesché, Sister M. Imelda Wallace, Rev. Gerald M. C. Fitzgerald, and Rev. Frederick Faber—to acquire a greater understanding of—and devotion to—the earthly father of Jesus. The discussion questions as well as the reflections on the virtues of St. Joseph lead children to apply the lessons of this saint's life to their own. The concluding section of this book contains prayers to St. Joseph, a short litany for children, prayers for the Nine First Wednesdays of St. Joseph, and an Act of Consecration to St. Joseph. As St. Teresa of Avila declared, "I wish I could persuade everyone to be devoted to this glorious saint!"

Alternative Book Reports for Catholic Students contains forty-five book report ideas to encourage critical thinking for ages seven to fourteen. These ideas are intended to provoke a reflection on those themes and topics that support and encourage Catholic living as well as some that may conflict with our Faith. Many report topics require an examination of our personal faith life and prompt us to take lessons from the saints to strengthen our own faith in God. The suggested activities vary from written exercises to creative art projects and include twenty-one topics specifically designed for saint biographies. Other activities can be used within a group or family.

Reading the Saints: Lists of Catholic Books for Children Plus Book Collecting Tips for the Home and School Library (formerly entitled *Saintly Resources*) is a valuable tool for Catholic home educators, classroom teachers, and collectors of Catholic juvenile books. *Reading the Saints* will help you discover living books from such popular out-of-print Catholic juvenile series as Catholic Treasury, Vision Books, and American Background Books as well as current series books for young Catholics. Use this book to find:

- Over 800 Catholic books listed by author, series, reading level, century, and geographical location

- More than 275 authors of saint biographies, historical fiction, and poetry written for Catholic juvenile readers

- Publishers of Catholic children's books, present and past

- Helpful advice for collecting and caring for used books

- Hundreds of age-appropriate, accessible living books to enrich your study of the Catholic Church's rich heritage of saints and notable Catholic historical figures

- Information on how to build and maintain your own library of Catholic juvenile books

- Inspiring quotations about book collecting, reading, and the love of books

The Outlaws of Ravenhurst Study Edition contains a classic story of the persecution of Scottish Catholics that was first written in 1923 and was revised and reprinted in 1950. This 2009 edition of Sr. M. Imelda Wallace's *Outlaws of Ravenhurst* contains the revised story of 1950 plus chapter-by-chapter aids to assist readers in assimilating the book's strong Catholic elements into their wn lives. The study section focuses on critical thinking, integration of biblical teachings, and the study of the virtuous life to which Christ calls us as mature Catholics. With its emphasis on virtues (theological and moral plus the gifts and fruits of the Holy Spirit), the spiritual and corporal works of mercy, and the Beatitudes, *Outlaws of Ravenhurst Study Edition* is a fun and effective catechetical tool for Catholics preparing for the Sacrament of Confirmation. (Also available as a study guide only)

The Family that Overtook Christ Study Edition: The Story of the Family of St. Bernard of Clairvaux is an excellent read for young adults who are preparing to receive the Sacrament of Confirmation. In this exciting chronicle of the life of twelfth-century knights, we have an entire family of nine saints who lay before us their individual means of achieving intimate union with Christ. Learn with the Fontaines family how to supernaturalize the natural, develop a God-consciousness, and attain sanctity by being yourself. Perfect for high-school read-aloud (or adult study), this new study edition has over 250 footnotes for increased comprehension and provides discussion/meditation points to promote the art of spiritual conversation. The appendix lists formulas of Catholic doctrine that are essential for confirmands not only to know but also to incorporate into their own spiritual lives.

A Confirmation Reader-Retreat: Read-Aloud Lessons, Stories and Poems for Young Catholics utilizes chapters from two excellent out-of-print Catholic books for children (*I Belong to God, Great Truths in Simple Stories for Children and Lovers of Children* by Lillian Clark; and *Children's Retreats in Preparation for First Confession, First Holy Communion, and Confirmation* by Rev. P.A. Halpin). This book provides a basic doctrinal review of the Sacrament of Confirmation as well as prayer experiences— a nine-day read-aloud retreat/novena. The reprinted material has been supplemented with short stories and poems that provide insights in applying catechetical doctrines to the daily life of young Catholics. Each lesson concludes with "I Talk with God"—a section that encourages readers (of all ages) to deepen their relationship with each of the Three Persons of the Blessed Trinity. Reflection questions promote the habit of spiritual conversation within your family—to encourage family members to discuss holy topics— and to help you grow together in holiness. Additionally, a traditional novena to the Holy Spirit is included.

To Order: Email info@RACEforHeaven.com or place an order from RACEforHeaven.com. Discover, MasterCard, VISA, PayPal, American Express, checks, and money orders are accepted.

9 781934 185445